101 Tips

on
Nutrition
for
People
with
Diabetes

Second Edition

Patti B. Geil, MS, RD, FADA, CDE
Lea Ann Holzmeister, RD, CDE

American
Diabetes
Association®

Cure • Care • Commitment®

Director, Book Publishing, Abe Ogden; *Managing Editor,* Greg Guthrie; *Editor,* Rebecca Lanning; *Production Manager,* Melissa Sprott; *Cover Design,* Naylor Design; *Printer,* Victor Graphics.

Printed in the United States of America
1 3 5 7 9 10 8 6 4 2

♾ The paper in this publication meets the requirements of the ANSI Standard Z39.48-1992 (permanence of paper).

ADA titles may be purchased for business or promotional use or for special sales. To purchase more than 50 copies of this book at a discount, or for custom editions of this book with your logo, contact the American Diabetes Association at the address below, at booksales@diabetes.org, or by calling 703-299-2046.

American Diabetes Association
1701 North Beauregard Street
Alexandria, Virginia 22311

To our families

Jeff, Erin, Adam, and Emily Holzmeister
Jack, Kristen, and Rachel Geil

101 thank-yous for your love and support!

—Lea Ann and Patti

Contents

Chapter 1   Nutrition: The Big Picture . 1

Chapter 2   Managing Medication 27

Chapter 3   Challenges of Children...... 37

Chapter 4   The Skinny on Fat............... 45

Chapter 5   How Sweet It Is..................... 59

Chapter 6   Food and Fitness 71

Chapter 7   Weighty Issues 81

Chapter 8   Off the Beaten Path 95

Chapter 9   Food for Thought 105

Chapter 10   Special Situations........... . . 115

Chapter 11   Nutrition Potpourri 129

Chapter 1
Nutrition:
The Big Picture

1 How do I know when I should see a registered dietitian?

See a registered dietitian (RD) when your diabetes is first diagnosed, when a new doctor changes your treatment plan, or twice a year for a routine review of your meal plan and goals. See the RD more often if

- You want to improve your diabetes management.
- Your have a lifestyle or schedule change, such as a new job, marriage, or pregnancy.
- Your nutritional needs keep changing (children).
- You've begun an exercise program or had a change in diabetes medication.
- You feel bored, frustrated, or unmotivated to use your meal plan.
- You have unexplained high and low blood glucose levels.
- You're concerned about your weight or blood fat levels.
- You develop nutrition-related complications, such as high blood pressure or kidney disease.

You may have an RD on your diabetes team. Ask your doctor or hospital for a referral. You can also call the American Diabetes Association (800-342-2383), the American Dietetic Association (800-877-1600), or the American Association of Diabetes Educators (800-338-3633) for referrals. Many RDs are certified diabetes educators (CDEs) and have additional training in diabetes care.

2 What should I eat until I can meet with the registered dietitian?

Eat the foods that are healthy for everyone—grains, beans, vegetables, fruits, low-fat milk, and meat. Cut down on foods and drinks with a lot of added sugar (soda, desserts, candy) and fat (fried foods, lunch meats, gravy, salad dressings). You do not need special or diet foods.

It is important to eat about the same amount of food at the same time each day. Don't eat one or two large meals. Try to eat at least three small meals each day, especially if you are taking diabetes medication. You may need a snack between meals and before you go to bed. Avoid drinking alcohol until you learn how it fits into your diabetes treatment plan. Remember, you can make a big difference in your diabetes management through what you choose to eat. Before you see the RD, keep a record of everything you eat and drink for 3–5 days and bring this record to your appointment. This will help the RD personalize the meal plan for you.

3 How often do I need to eat to keep my blood glucose levels near normal?

This depends on the type of diabetes you have, your medications, the amount of physical activity you get, and where your blood glucose level is at the moment. An RD can help you decide.

For people with type 1 or people with type 2 who use insulin: Have food in your system when your insulin is peaking. You may need three meals and an evening snack. If you take two injections of short- and intermediate-acting insulin, you may need three meals and three snacks. If you use rapid-acting insulin, eat within 15 minutes of taking your insulin. You may need a snack for physical activity (see page 74). A common mistake is not waiting a half hour to eat after taking regular insulin. If you start eating before insulin activity is peaking, you may have higher blood glucose levels after meals.

For people with type 2: Eat a small meal every 2–3 hours. When you eat smaller amounts of food, your blood glucose levels are lower after eating. Mini-meals spread throughout the day may help control your hunger and calorie intake, leading to near-normal blood glucose levels and weight loss. Your blood cholesterol levels will also be lower.

4 What can I eat for snacks?

Choose from the same healthy foods that you eat at meals. Often, snacks are based on foods with 15 grams of carbohydrate per serving. Choose foods from the grain group, such as air-popped popcorn, baked tortilla chips and salsa, graham crackers, whole grain crackers, pretzels, bagels, or cereal. Fresh fruits and vegetables make excellent snacks, and they're also portable! To make a snack more substantial, add a source of low-fat protein, such as low-fat or skim milk, reduced-fat peanut butter on a slice of whole wheat bread or a bagel, low-fat cheese on whole wheat crackers, or a slice of turkey breast on whole-wheat bread. Keep in mind, however, that although adding protein to your snack may ward off hunger, it does not increase blood glucose to prevent hypoglycemia, and it may add unwanted calories.

Be prepared! Always carry a snack with you in case of a delayed meal or unexpected change in your schedule. Snacks can be stashed in your desk, brief-case, backpack, or glove compartment. Having good food on hand will save you from hypoglycemia and from having to settle for less nutritious fast foods.

5 How can keeping a food diary help my diabetes?

The food you eat raises your blood glucose. Until you write it down, you probably are not aware of how much or what you are eating. A food diary helps you make important decisions about your medication, meal plan, and exercise plan.

- Record information you need. If you want to lose weight, measure your serving sizes and write down how many calories or fat grams you're getting for several days. Looking up the nutrient values of foods helps you learn what nutrients each food gives you.
- Keep records that are easy to use—a notebook, calendar, or form created on your computer. Write it down when you eat it; don't wait until later.
- Use the information. Bring your record to the next appointment with your RD. Look for patterns in your eating behaviors and blood glucose levels. For example, your records may show that high-fat snacks in late afternoon result in high blood glucose at dinner. Or you may notice that when your lunch is much smaller than other meals you are too hungry before dinner. You may want to adjust the size of lunch and decrease your afternoon eating.

Research shows that individuals who keep food and activity records are more successful in following their meal plan.

6 Why are serving sizes important? Is there an easy way to remember them?

No matter what meal plan you follow—carbohydrate counting, exchanges, or the food guide pyramid—serving size is the key. An extra ounce of meat or a tablespoon of margarine doesn't sound like much, but it can quickly add up to higher blood glucose levels and weight gain.

Begin by using standard kitchen measuring cups, spoons, and food scales until you train your eyes to see correct serving sizes. Once you've weighed, measured, and looked at 1/2 cup of green beans or 5 oz of chicken, you'll have a mental picture no matter where you dine. Every few months, measure some servings again to keep your eyes sharp and your servings the right size.

Mental pictures can help you eat correct serving sizes.

Food	Looks like
1 cup pasta or rice	a clenched fist
1/2 cup vegetables	half a tennis ball
1 cup broccoli	a light bulb
3 oz meat, chicken, or fish	a deck of cards or the palm of a woman's hand
1 oz cheese	two saltine crackers or a 1-inch-square cube

7 What should I be looking for on food labels—carbohydrate or fat?

Most people with diabetes should be looking at both carbohydrate and fat on the Nutrition Facts panel on food labels. Carbohydrate is what raises your blood glucose the most, so it's important to you. Fat carries the most calories per gram, so it affects your weight. Also, diabetes puts you more at risk for developing heart disease. Eating foods lower in fat (especially saturated fat and trans fat) may help you lose weight and lower your risk for heart disease.

The total amount of carbohydrate and the type of carbohydrate you eat can affect your blood glucose. The carbohydrate listed in the Nutrition Facts can be from beans, vegetables, pasta, grains, and sugars (added or naturally present in foods such as milk and fruit). The food label will tell you exactly how many grams of carbohydrate and fat are in a serving of food.

8 How do I deal with comments such as, "Are you allowed to eat that?"

Your family and friends mean well. Here are some strategies for you to use when others seem to be overly concerned with what you're eating and drinking:

- **Recognize your own feelings.** Part of adjusting to diabetes is recognizing the difficult emotions that come with it. How do you feel about the lifestyle changes and pressures of self-care?
- **Recognize the feelings of family and friends.** Your family and friends are also adjusting to your diabetes and the ways it affects them. They may feel anxious, intimidated, guilty, or overwhelmed.
- **Use positive reframing.** Change the way you see the situation. If you feel angry at someone's comment, take a moment to acknowledge your own feeling and then the other person's feeling. Then look at the situation in a positive way. For example, you may say, "Thanks for reminding me. I know you want to help. I've already planned to adjust my insulin (or exercise) to handle the additional calories and carbohydrate in this food."
- **Develop an interaction plan.** Changing years of old thinking and communication patterns takes time. In a calm moment, discuss a new way to talk about food and diabetes issues.

9 Now that sugar is no longer forbidden for people with diabetes, can I eat all the sweets I want?

It's true that the carbohydrate in table sugar can have the same effect on your blood glucose as any other carbohydrate, such as that in bread, potatoes, or fruit. Different carbohydrates do raise blood glucose in different ways; however, for blood glucose management, it's more important to focus on the total amount of carbohydrate you eat, rather than on where it comes from. You substitute sweets into your meal plan for other carbohydrates—don't add them on top.

No, don't have sweets at every meal. Sugary foods don't have the nutrients, vitamins, and minerals that your body needs to be healthy. That's why we call these calories "empty" and list these foods as extras in the food pyramid. If you include sweets in a meal, eat a small serving and check your blood glucose before and 1–2 hours after you eat to see how it affects you. Keep an eye on your weight and blood glucose levels over time. Hold back on the sweets if you see your numbers creeping up.

10 I went to lunch with three friends who also have diabetes. We all follow different types of meal plans. What happened to the "diabetic" diet?

Just as there is no one medication that works for all people with diabetes, there is no single meal-planning approach. The standard 1,800-calorie preprinted diet sheet is gone. Individualization is the key to effective diabetes management.

The best meal plans are designed by you and an RD and are based on your health, other medications, activity level, and treatment goals. Your friend with type 1 diabetes may be taking multiple insulin injections and using the carbohydrate counting approach with frequent blood glucose monitoring. Her food choices would be quite different from those of your friend with type 2 diabetes who has high blood fat levels and needs to lose weight. She may be trying to lower her carbohydrate intake and increase the monounsaturated fats in her diet by eating more nuts, olives, or canola oil. And the friend who works a swing shift is probably using an entirely different approach to the timing and food choices in her meals and snacks. The important thing is to use a meal plan that works for you.

11 I've heard that a low-carbohydrate, high-protein, high-fat diet will help me lose weight without cutting calories. Should I change from the high-carbohydrate, low-fat diet I've always followed?

Probably not. A low-carbohydrate diet is very difficult to follow for a long period of time. On this diet, you eat meat, eggs, and cheese but very few carbohydrate foods, such as pasta, breads, fruits, and vegetables. You eat too few fruits and vegetables to get all the vitamins and minerals you need.

The rapid weight loss on a low-carbohydrate diet comes from an unhealthy loss of water and muscle tissue. Side effects include dehydration, low blood pressure, and increased work for the kidneys. The high-fat foods certainly aren't good for heart health. Other side effects include constipation, fatigue, and nausea. And as with all very restricted diets, once you go back to a normal way of eating, your weight is going to come back.

Until there's more evidence, it's probably best to continue with a balanced carbohydrate meal plan. If you have insulin resistance, you may do better substituting some monounsaturated fats for carbohydrates (see page 53). Get your health care team's help to decide on a nutrition approach for you.

12 Will fiber help my diabetes management?

Fiber can keep your blood glucose from going high after a meal because it slows down the speed at which the food is digested. Foods that are high in fiber are good sources of vitamins, minerals, and other substances important for good health. A high-fiber, low-fat way of eating can also reduce your risk for cancer, cardiovascular disease, high blood pressure, and obesity. Fiber has a favorable effect on blood cholesterol, too.

Fiber in food is made up of two types: insoluble fiber, such as that in vegetables and whole-grain products, and soluble fiber, found in fruits, oats, barley, and beans. Insoluble fiber improves gastrointestinal function, while soluble fiber can affect blood glucose and cholesterol. Unfortunately, most Americans eat only 8–10 grams of fiber daily, not the recommended 20–35 grams a day from a variety of foods. You can increase fiber by eating foods such as the ones in this chart.

Food	Serving Size	Total Fiber (g)	Soluble Fiber (g)
Beans	1/2 cup cooked	6.9	2.8
Oat bran	1/3 cup dry	4.0	2.0
Barley	1/4 cup dry	3.0	0.9
Orange, fresh	1 small	2.9	1.8
Oatmeal	1/3 cup dry	2.7	1.4

13 Is it true that beans can improve diabetes management?

Yes. Beans are very high in carbohydrates and need to be eaten in the proper portions, but beans digest slowly, resulting in only a small rise in blood glucose and insulin levels. Several research studies have shown that eating 1 1/2–2 1/2 cups of cooked beans daily has a beneficial effect on diabetes management. Beans also reduce the risk of cardiovascular disease, a common complication for people with diabetes. Eating 1–3 cups of cooked beans a day will lower total cholesterol by 5–19%. Beans are also an excellent source of folate, which may help reduce the risk of cardiovascular disease.

Packed with protein, fiber, vitamins, and minerals, beans are also low in fat, cholesterol, and sodium. They can be included in all types of diabetes meal plans. Beans can be used in salads, soups, or entrées. Canned beans require less preparation time and have the same beneficial effects as dried beans, but they are higher in sodium than beans "cooked from scratch."

Soak dried beans overnight and rinse well before cooking. Introduce beans gradually into your diet, chew them thoroughly, and drink plenty of liquids to aid digestion. Enzyme products such as "Beano" can also help you avoid gastrointestinal distress.

14 I keep hearing about carbohydrate counting. Is it still okay to use exchanges?

Yes. The exchange system is a valuable way for people with diabetes to plan meals. It can also help if you want to count carbohydrates. The Exchange Lists for Meal Planning group foods with similar carbohydrate content, so the "carb" counting is already done for you. For example, all the foods on the starch list (1 slice of bread, 3/4 cup dry cereal, etc.) contain 15 grams of carbohydrate.

To use exchanges, you need an individualized meal plan that tells you how many exchanges from each list to eat daily for meals and snacks. You can choose a variety of foods from the exchange lists to fit into your meal plan. An RD can help you design a meal plan and teach you how to use this system. In 2003, the Exchange Lists were updated. The food groupings were changed and more foods were included. A pocket-sized guide is now available.

Many people prefer to use exchanges because it helps keep their food choices balanced and healthy. If this system works for you, there is no reason to switch to another.

15 What is carbohydrate counting?

Carbohydrate counting is a precise method of meal planning for people with diabetes. Foods containing carbohydrate (grains, vegetables, fruit, milk, and sugar) have the largest effect on blood glucose levels. A small amount of carbohydrate (1 apple) raises blood glucose some; a larger amount of carbohydrate (3 apples) raises blood glucose more. You track how the carbohydrate affects you by monitoring your blood glucose. You'll have to invest some time in monitoring blood glucose, record keeping, measuring food servings, and learning about nutrients in foods.

Carbohydrate counting has two levels: basic and advanced. Basic carbohydrate counting is generally used by people with type 2 diabetes and consists mostly of counting and eating consistent amounts of carbohydrate. Advanced carbohydrate counting is often used by people taking insulin and is based on recognizing and managing patterns in blood glucose, food, medication, and exercise for intensive management of blood glucose. You may only need to learn about basic carbohydrate counting. The amount of work may seem overwhelming at first, but most people find that the improvements in their blood glucose levels are worth it! An RD can help you learn about carbohydrate counting.

16 Do I need special vitamins and minerals because I have diabetes?

You don't need special vitamins because of diabetes. You do need vitamins and minerals for a well-functioning body, whether you have diabetes or not. If you are eating a variety of foods, you don't need a special vitamin or mineral supplement. There is currently no scientific evidence to show that certain vitamins or minerals can improve your blood glucose management, except in rare cases of deficiencies of the minerals chromium, copper, magnesium, manganese, selenium, or zinc (see pages 97–99).

Discuss your diet with your physician or RD. You may need a vitamin and mineral supplement if you are

- on a diet of fewer than 1,200 calories a day
- following a strict vegetarian diet
- at risk for bone disease
- over age 65
- pregnant or breastfeeding
- taking diuretics
- having trouble keeping your blood glucose levels on target

17 I really don't feel like eating in the morning. Do I have to eat breakfast?

Yes. Breakfast is crucial for people with diabetes. Your body has been without food for 8–12 hours. If you have type 1 diabetes, you need food to balance your injected insulin. If you have type 2 diabetes, you may skip breakfast to cut calories and lose weight, but it can lead to overeating later. In fact, research shows that breakfast skippers have higher blood cholesterol levels and extra pounds!

The best breakfast has carbohydrate, protein, and fiber. Save high-fat foods like bacon, sausage, and eggs for special occasions. You can choose whole-grain cereal or an English muffin, low-fat milk or yogurt, and fruit, but there's no rule that says breakfast can't be whole-wheat pasta tossed with low-fat ricotta cheese or a leftover chicken breast with a piece of fruit.

Once you experience the dividends that breakfast pays in mood, performance, and diabetes management, you'll never skip your morning meal again!

Hint: People who eat a smaller evening meal (and spread their calories out over the day) are more likely to wake up hungry for breakfast.

18 I've heard I'm supposed to eat five fruits and vegetables a day. Why?

Increasing the fruit and vegetables in your diet may lead to better health, particularly in the prevention of cancer and heart disease. Fruits and vegetables are low in fat and are rich sources of vitamin A, vitamin C, and fiber. The average American eats only one serving of fruit and two servings of vegetables a day. You can find ways to put five or more servings in your salads, soups, sandwiches, main dishes, and snacks.

Fruits and vegetables affect diabetes in different ways. Fruit has 15 grams of carbohydrate per serving and affects your blood glucose within 2 hours. The amount your blood glucose rises depends on whether you eat the fruit on an empty stomach, the form of the fruit (cooked or raw, whole or juice), and your blood glucose level when you eat. Check your blood glucose level after eating fruit to see what it does to you. Nonstarchy vegetables contain only 5 grams of carbohydrate per serving, few calories, and lots of vitamins and minerals. Moderate portions of vegetables have little effect on blood glucose but major effects on your health. Eat up!

19 Why does it seem that I need less food—and enjoy it less—now that I'm older?

If you are not as active as you were when you were younger, you probably don't need to eat as many calories. However, it may be that your appetite and enjoyment are being affected by changes in one of the following:

- Taste buds—affecting taste and interest in food
- Smell—affecting interest in food and the amount you eat
- Vision—making it difficult to read labels or recipes
- Hearing—affecting your ability to enjoy the social events around eating
- Touch—making it difficult to prepare food
- Teeth or poorly fitting dentures—making it painful to eat anything but soft, easy-to-chew foods

For reasons such as these, you may skip meals or eat fewer calories than you need, which affects your diabetes management. Limitations on movement can keep you from exercising, leading to loss of energy and appetite. Poor nutrition itself can bring on fatigue and a general sense of not feeling well. Work with your RD to overcome any challenges to following your meal plan.

20 Are plant sources of protein better for me than animal protein?

Maybe. Plant proteins have benefits for people with diabetes. Plant foods are low in fat, especially saturated fat, and high in fiber. Animal protein adds cholesterol and saturated fat to our diets. People with diabetes have a greater risk of heart disease earlier in life; therefore, it is important to decrease your intake of saturated fat and cholesterol. For people with diabetic kidney disease, changing the source of protein in the diet is being studied as a treatment. Whether plant protein (beans, nuts, vegetables, tofu) is preferred over animal protein (meat, poultry, fish, milk, eggs) has not been decided. Discuss the latest research with your diabetes care professionals. We do know that people in other countries who eat less meat and more soy protein and rice have lower rates of cancer and heart disease than Americans, who eat lots of animal protein.

Animal protein contains all eight essential amino acids that you need to build cells in the body. Because your body can't make them, your food choices must supply them. However, eating a variety of plant proteins each day can also provide all the amino acids that you need (see page 24).

21 Is there a benefit to including more soy foods in my diet?

Yes. Soy foods are low in saturated fat, have no cholesterol, and contain high-quality protein. Scientists are learning about compounds in soybeans that may reduce your risk of certain chronic diseases, such as heart disease, osteoporosis, and cancer. Eating soy foods may lower blood cholesterol levels and decrease your risk for heart disease. Soy protein contains a group of phytochemicals called isoflavones that may directly lower blood cholesterol levels. In certain stages of kidney disease, vegetable protein may be easier on the kidneys than animal protein.

Soybeans are included in a variety of foods, from ice cream to burgers, and they can be eaten whole or used in your recipes.

Soy Food	Serving Size	Calories	Carbohydrate (g)	Protein (g)	Isoflavones (mg)
Soybeans	1/2 cup, cooked	149	9	14	35
Tempeh	1/2 cup	165	14	16	40
Tofu	1/2 cup	94	2	10	40
Soy nuts	1 oz	128	9	11	40
Soy milk	1/2 cup	40	2	3	40
Miso	2 Tbsp	72	10	4	10

22 Should I eat less protein to keep my kidneys healthy?

Not necessarily. The American Diabetes Association recommends that you eat the same amount of protein as the general public. The Recommended Daily Allowance suggests that healthy adults eat 15–20% of their daily calories as protein or about 0.8 grams of protein per kilogram of weight. For a 132-pound person, this would be about 50 grams of protein per day. Some plant and animal protein choices are listed below. Individuals whose blood glucose levels are not on target may benefit from more protein than the RDA recommended amount. However, most Americans eat more than enough protein. If you already have kidney disease, you may want to eat less protein. Your doctor will consider the stage of kidney disease and your overall nutrition before prescribing a low-protein diet.

Animal Proteins	Protein (g)
1 oz lean meat, poultry, fish	7
1 cup milk or yogurt	8
1 egg	7
Plant Proteins	**Protein (g)**
1/2 cup cooked lentils, peas, beans	7
2 Tbsp peanut butter	8
1/3 cup nuts	7
4 oz tofu	7
1 slice bread, 1/2 cup rice	2–3

23 How can I use the USDA's MyPyramid system to eat healthfully for diabetes?

The United States Department of Agriculture has replaced the Food Guide Pyramid with MyPyramid, a system based on the 2005 Dietary Guidelines. This system emphasizes an individual approach to healthy food choices and physical activity and has a new pyramid-shaped graphic or symbol to illustrate its key concepts. The MyPyramid system recommends foods high in vitamins, minerals, dietary fiber, and other essential nutrients while limiting foods high in saturated fat, trans fat, and cholesterol. This system also promotes balancing calorie intake with energy needs to achieve a healthy weight. You can use the online MyPyramid system at www. MyPyramid.gov to create an individual pyramid based on your age, sex, and physical activity level. This site also helps you assess your current eating habits and physical activity.

The key nutrition concepts in the Dietary Guidelines and the MyPyramid system are the basis for a healthy eating plan for diabetes, which is the first step in diabetes meal planning. MyPyramid is designed to encourage you to include more foods in your diet from grains, vegetables, and fruits—and fewer foods from fats and foods high in discretionary calories. Foods high in discretionary calories include foods with added sugars, solid fats, and alcohol. Healthy eating for diabetes emphasizes the same principles.

Chapter 2
Managing Medication

24 Do I need to eat snacks now that I'm taking diabetes pills?

The way your pills work tells you whether you need snacks. Diabetes pills called *sulfonylureas* help the pancreas secrete insulin and can cause low blood glucose. If you take chlorpropamide (Diabinese), tolazamide (Tolinase), tolbutamide (Orinase), glipizide (Glucotrol), glyburide (DiaBeta, Micronase, or Glynase), or glimepiride (Amaryl), you probably need snacks, especially in the afternoon and evening.

Biguanides (Glucophage) help your body use insulin and decrease how much glucose your body makes and absorbs, so you don't need snacks. *Alpha-glucosidase inhibitors* (Precose and Glyset) delay absorption of glucose and do not cause hypoglycemia, so you don't need a snack. If you take these medications with another diabetes medication and have low blood glucose, treat it with glucose tablets or milk. Acarbose slows the breakdown of sugar and may prevent your blood glucose from rising. *Meglitinides* (Starlix and Prandin) help the pancreas release insulin and are taken with meals or large (250-calorie or more) snacks. Snacks at other times are not necessary. *Thiazolidinediones* (Actos and Avandia) make the body more sensitive to insulin; snacks are not needed.

Some diabetes pills are combinations of two medications; use the above precautions for those drugs. If you take insulin and diabetes pills, you will probably need to eat healthy snacks to match the peak action of your insulin.

TYPE 2

25 Can I adjust my diet to avoid the side effects of acarbose (Precose)?

Acarbose is a pill for type 2 diabetes that slows down the digestion of carbohydrates. This helps lower your blood glucose level after a meal. It is often used along with another kind of diabetes pill and is taken three times a day with meals.

Acarbose may cause gas, diarrhea, and abdominal pain. This is because the carbohydrate you eat is not completely digested. It may help to increase the amount of medication slowly over a period of months. Temporarily eating a low-fiber diet may also help. Avoid seeds, nuts, or beans. Select low-fiber cereals, breads, pasta, and rice. Peel and seed fruits and vegetables. It may also help to avoid gas-forming foods, such as beans and vegetables in the cabbage family. Other foods that may cause gas are milk, wheat germ, onions, carrots, celery, bananas, raisins, dried apricots, prune juice, and sorbitol, a sugar alcohol used as a sweetener.

26 My doctor wants me to start insulin, but I'm afraid I'll gain too much weight. How can I prevent weight gain while I'm taking insulin?

When your blood glucose is high, you lose calories as sugar in your urine. Taking insulin will help you manage your blood glucose levels, which can make you feel better every day and lower your chances of developing complications. This is important! However, when you stop losing calories in your urine, you can gain weight. Review your eating habits, your total calories, the types of food you eat, and the amount of fat and carbohydrate you eat with your RD. You may not need to eat as many calories, or you may need more exercise. These changes will help you take advantage of the more efficient job your body is doing at capturing and storing glucose.

Insulin can cause weight gain in another way. If you take more insulin than you need, then you have to eat to "feed" the insulin and avoid low blood glucose. If you find yourself eating more than you want just to avoid hypoglycemia, your insulin dose may need adjusting.

TYPE 1 & TYPE 2

27 My doctor just switched my insulin to Humalog. How will this affect my blood glucose and meal plan?

You may find it easier to keep your blood glucose levels on target, and you may have more flexible mealtimes. Humalog is a rapid-acting insulin that starts working within 10 minutes and peaks in 30–90 minutes, the way a normal pancreas responds to food. You may not need snacks between meals as you did with regular insulin, because rapid-acting insulin does not stay in your body as long. You may need less Humalog than your regular insulin dose but more intermediate- or long-acting insulin.

When you take a rapid-acting insulin and your blood glucose is in the target range, you must eat within 15 minutes. This is quite different from waiting 30–45 minutes with regular insulin. If your blood glucose level is low before your meal, you might take Humalog after your meal.

It is easier to fine-tune your insulin dose to a meal with rapid-acting insulin, because it works only on the food eaten right then. Monitor your blood glucose levels when you begin using Humalog to learn how the medication works for you.

28 Whenever I eat pizza, my blood glucose level goes high. What can I do about that?

You might try eating a smaller serving. The type of crust, sauce, toppings, and size of slice vary a lot, so it is easy to overeat pizza. When you order pizza, ask for nutrition information. If you purchase it in the grocery store, check the Nutrition Facts panel. Exercising after you eat pizza can help bring down your blood glucose level.

For some people, high blood glucose occurs several hours after eating, perhaps because pizza is digested at different rates. Each person has a unique response to each food. Monitor your blood glucose for up to 9 hours after eating pizza to find your response. If you take insulin, increasing premeal rapid-acting insulin may not be enough. Your intermediate- or long-acting insulin may need an adjustment also. Talk with your health care providers.

If you take diabetes pills, count the carbohydrates in your pizza serving. Is this more than you usually eat? Monitor your blood glucose before and after eating to find your response.

TYPE 1 & TYPE 2

29 What is a carbohydrate-to-insulin ratio? Can I use this to eat what I want?

A carbohydrate-to-insulin ratio is used by people who manage diabetes with insulin. The relationship between the food you eat and the insulin you take can be shown as a ratio—a carbohydrate-to-insulin ratio. This ratio tells you how much rapid-acting insulin to use, which is very useful when you eat more (or less) carbohydrate than usual. You have more flexibility in food choices and timing of meals. Take care, however, to choose foods that give you the nutrients you need, and don't overindulge. To figure the insulin dose, you also take into account any exercise that you do. For most people, a typical carbohydrate-to-insulin ratio is 1 to 15; that is, you need one unit of insulin for each 15 grams of carbohydrate you eat. Your carbohydrate-to-insulin ratio varies according to the meal or time of day. Many people have a lower carbohydrate-to-insulin ratio at breakfast than at dinner. The amount of fat, protein, and fiber in the meal will also affect the insulin's action. Blood glucose monitoring helps you adjust the ratio for different kinds of meals and mealtimes. Diabetes professionals can help you determine whether this approach will work for you.

30 I've heard about a new medication called Byetta. I know it's an injection; is it insulin?

Byetta is an injectable, prescription-only medication for type 2 diabetes that may help to improve blood glucose management in those who take metformin, a sulfonylurea, or both. Byetta is not insulin, but it enhances insulin secretion in the presence of high blood glucose. It helps stop the liver from producing too much glucose and slows down the rate at which glucose enters the bloodstream. Byetta may cause you to feel less hungry and eat less, leading to weight loss. Mild nausea is one potential side effect of Byetta, but this usually disappears in 4–8 weeks. Because you may eat less, low blood glucose can occur if you take Byetta in combination with a sulfonylurea.

Byetta comes in its own prefilled pen and should be taken an hour before eating.

Chapter 3
Challenges of Children

31 How often should my child have sweets?

Occasionally. Sweets are called "extras" or "discretionary calories" in MyPyramid, which means you can enjoy them when your nutrient needs from the other five groups have been met. If your child eats ice cream, cookies, and candy often or in large amounts, he or she won't have room for the foods he or she really needs. Some experts recommend offering sweets as part of a meal, so that children won't think of sweets as "special." Having sweets in appropriate amounts as part of the meal plan may also keep children from feeling guilty about eating them. This approach teaches children that high-sugar foods are part of the carbohydrates in the meal plan, instead of an addition to it.

Many kid-friendly foods that may seem healthy have nutrient values similar to candy or desserts. A fruit snack pouch is handy but may contain 100% sugar with only fruit flavoring. Look closely at labels to see how much of the carbohydrate content is sugar. A juicy piece of fresh fruit is also handy, and it supplies essential vitamins, minerals, and dietary fiber.

32 What should I do if my toddler refuses to eat his or her meal?

If you gave insulin before the meal, give your child a peanut butter and jelly sandwich or milk or a bigger portion of a food you know she or he will eat to cover the insulin given and prevent low blood glucose.

It is not uncommon for a toddler to refuse to eat. This situation can make parents anxious, especially if rapid- or short-acting insulin has already been given. Keep in mind that during the toddler stage, growth and appetite are slowing down, and your child is becoming an independent self-feeder. Your toddler may be eating adult table foods but is not ready for adult-size servings. Are you serving appropriate types and amounts of foods? Is your child joining the family in a regular schedule of meals and snacks? Be sure your child has enough time between meals and snacks so that he or she will have an appetite. In some cases, you can give rapid-acting insulin after the meal and adjust the dose to the amount of food the child has eaten.

33 What if my child is napping and it's time for a snack?

If your child's nap will pass snack time, you might test his or her blood glucose if your child is not startled and awakened by the finger stick. Some children sleep through a stick. However, waking your child this way may be too traumatic. It may be better to simply wake your child and feed him or her.

For very young children, preventing low blood glucose is your goal. Low blood glucose levels are dangerous because they can affect the developing brain. Know your child's insulin types and doses and understand when they peak and how long they keep acting. You have to learn to balance the amount and type of insulin with food and eating times.

Discuss the following approaches to nap time snacks with your diabetes professionals:

- If your child's nap is 30 minutes to 1 hour after a meal, you don't need to test blood glucose or feed him or her before the nap.
- If your child's snack is scheduled for 3:00 p.m. and nap starts at 2:00 p.m., offer part of the snack before the nap and the rest after the nap.

34 Is it okay for my child to eat school lunches?

Probably. School lunches can fit into your child's meal plan, but you'll have to do some homework. Review menus with your child and select those that your child likes. Evaluate foods and serving sizes with your child's food and insulin plan in mind. Often, the cafeteria staff or your child must adjust the serving size. Food items may need to be added by the cafeteria or brought from home by your child, and some food items (sweetened fruit, fruit punch, or desserts) may need to be left off the tray.

Your child's comfort level with making changes in the menu, which may single him or her out as different, could cause a problem. Also, how willing are school personnel to work with you? A change in the menu may complicate things. Help your child learn how to choose basic foods. In junior high and high school, menu choices are more varied but may not be as healthy. Review nutrition information from fast-food restaurants with your child to help him or her select foods that fit the meal plan. Carrying a lunch from home part of the time can help balance meals.

35 How do I handle trick-or-treating or other holiday activities for my child with diabetes?

Part of growing up with diabetes is learning to make decisions about eating in special situations. Deciding with your child when, what kind, and how much candy he or she will eat can help form positive attitudes and feelings. If you talk with your child, you may find that food or treats are not what is most important to him or her about holiday activities.

Read the Nutrition Facts label on candy with your child and discuss the nutritional value of candy. Help your child make adjustments to the meal plan to include favorite treats from time to time. Some Halloween candy can be put in the freezer for later, if your child is not tempted by having it in the house. Discuss how to carefully monitor blood glucose . If your child takes insulin, ask your diabetes team to explain the option of adjusting insulin upward to cover extra treats. Other family members can help by offering to trade some of the child's candy for money, movie passes, sleepovers, staying up late, or use of a big brother or sister's stereo. Plan ahead to prevent frustration and disappointment.

36 Should my child follow a special diet for type 2 diabetes?

Making changes in lifestyle, including diet and physical activity changes, is the most important treatment strategy for children with type 2 diabetes. However, this does not mean that your child should start a "diet." Meals and snacks that are healthy for children with type 2 diabetes are healthy for the whole family. Start by scheduling your family's meals and snacks at about the same time each day and avoid skipping meals. Provide healthy food choices, such as whole grains, fruits, vegetables, and low-fat meat and dairy foods. Choose high-fat, high-sugar foods, such as fried foods, lunch meats, desserts, and high-sugar drinks, less often. Help your child eat the right amount at meals and snacks to keep blood glucose in balance. Serve child-size portions at meals and snacks.

If your child is overweight, talk with your doctor or registered dietitian about helping your child lose weight safely. Like adults, children must take in less food than their bodies burn for energy to lose weight. At least 60 minutes of physical activity every day will help keep blood glucose levels in the normal range and will help burn extra calories.

Chapter 4
The Skinny on Fat

37 What should my cholesterol levels be? What is the difference between "good" and "bad" cholesterol?

The ADA recommends that people with diabetes have their blood lipids checked every year. A lipid profile measures the levels of high-density lipoprotein (HDL), low-density lipoprotein (LDL), and triglycerides. HDL (good) cholesterol carries cholesterol from every part of the body back to the liver for disposal. If you have high levels of HDL cholesterol (higher than 40 mg/dl for men or 50 mg/dl for women), you are less likely to have heart disease. LDL (bad) cholesterol carries cholesterol from the liver to other tissues. Along the way, it forms deposits on the walls of arteries and other blood vessels. High levels of LDL cholesterol (above 100 mg/dl) show an increased risk of heart disease. Your body stores extra fat and calories as triglycerides. Good triglyceride levels are less than 150 mg/dl.

Blood Lipid Goals for People with Diabetes	
LDL (bad) Cholesterol	<100 mg/dl
HDL (good) Cholesterol	>40 mg/dl (men)
	>50 mg/dl (women)
Triglycerides	<150 mg/dl

SOURCE: ADA Clinical Practice Recommendations 2006

38 How much can changes in diet lower my blood cholesterol level?

Diet changes may decrease your LDL (bad) cholesterol by 15–25 mg/dl. For every 1% decrease in your total cholesterol, you decrease your risk for heart disease by 2%. Wouldn't you rather improve your risk factors for heart disease without medications, using diet changes only?

A heart-healthy eating plan is low in saturated fat and dietary cholesterol with total fat around 25–35% of total calories. This helps reduce blood cholesterol. Eating foods containing more fiber, such as beans, can also help reduce blood levels of cholesterol (see page 15). An RD can help you find the best amount of fat, carbohydrate, and protein in your food choices to lower your cholesterol, maintain a healthy weight, and manage your blood glucose levels.

The following suggestions can help you eat low-fat meals:

- Select lean meats and cook with little or no fat.
- Choose low-fat or fat-free milk products.
- Eat less meat, cheese, and bacon.
- Eat low-fat breads and starchy foods, such as potatoes, rice, and beans.
- Remember that sweets, such as pastries and chocolate, are often also high in fat.

39 Is it more important to decrease the cholesterol or the saturated fat in my diet?

Focus on the saturated fat. Decreasing saturated fat in your diet has a more significant effect on your blood cholesterol level. Saturated fats come mainly from animal foods, such as meat, poultry, butter, and whole milk, and from coconut, palm, and palm kernel oils. Foods high in saturated fats are firm at room temperature.

To eat less saturated fat, use liquid vegetable oils instead of shortening, margarine, or butter whenever you can. Cut back on total fat and you'll likely reduce saturated fats, too. Check for saturated fat on the Nutrition Facts panels on food labels. Check the ingredient list also. A food labeled "low in saturated fat" must contain one gram or less of saturated fat per serving and no more than 15% of calories from saturated fat.

Your liver makes most of the cholesterol in your body, but every cell can also make cholesterol. When the body makes too much, the risk for heart disease goes up. Cholesterol also comes from animal foods. Cholesterol is found in milk, meat, poultry, eggs, fish, and dairy foods. However, dietary cholesterol doesn't automatically become blood cholesterol.

40 How can I boost good (HDL) cholesterol and lower bad (LDL) cholesterol?

To increase HDL cholesterol and lower LDL cholesterol
- Stay physically active. Exercise helps keep HDL levels normal, reduces blood pressure, helps control stress, helps control body weight, gives your heart muscle a good workout, and helps keep blood glucose levels on target.
- Lose weight.
- Reduce the fat in your diet to about 30% of calories from fat and 7% from saturated fat. Replace some saturated fat in your diet with monounsaturated fats.
- Stop smoking. Smoking may lower HDL cholesterol levels and is a key factor in sudden death from cardiovascular disease. Smoking seems to raise blood pressure and heart rate and may increase the tendency of blood to clot, which can lead to a heart attack.

Other ways to decrease your LDL cholesterol are to
- Keep your blood glucose levels as close to normal as possible. This may decrease your LDL cholesterol by up to 10–15%.
- Eat high-fiber foods, such as beans, oatmeal, oat bran, wheat bran, barley, and some fruits and vegetables. They contain soluble fiber, which seems to lower LDL cholesterol levels.

41 How do I know if I'm eating the right amount of fat?

Talk to an RD about the right amount of fat for you, based on your weight and blood glucose and lipid goals. Most people eat too much fat. Fats contain 9 calories per gram, which means they contain a lot of calories in a small amount of food.

Write down what you eat for a few days, including the fat grams in your foods. The Nutrition Facts panel on food labels gives this information. For most people, fat should contribute about 30% of total calories for the day. Here is how to figure the number of grams of fat to eat if 30% of your 1,800 calories come from fat: 1,800 x 0.30 = 540 calories from fat. Then, find the number of fat grams in 540 calories (9 calories per 1 gram of fat): 540 ÷ 9 = 60 grams of fat per day.

Total Calories	Fat (g) for 30% of Calories
1,200	40
1,500	50
1,800	60
2,100	70
2,400	80
2,600	87

42 Can I have an unlimited amount of fat-free foods?

No. Fat-free does not mean the food is calorie-free or carbohydrate-free. Nor does it mean that it is a "free food." A free food is a term used by people with diabetes for foods that have less than 20 calories or less than 5 grams of carbohydrate per serving.

Fat-free foods have fat taken out and sometimes replaced by fat replacers. Some fat replacers, such as those used in fat-free salad dressings, contain carbohydrate and can affect your blood glucose level. Also, many fat-free foods have more sugar added to them for taste, and this will affect your blood glucose level.

If your weight and blood lipids are in a healthy range, you don't need fat-free foods. If your goal is to lower blood lipids and lose weight, moderate portions of some fat-free foods may help you. Read the Nutrition Facts on food labels to get the serving size, calories, and carbohydrate content to help you decide how fat-free foods fit into your meal plan.

43 How can I eat more monounsaturated fats?

Use olive oil, canola oil, or nuts in your meals. The ADA recommends that you replace part of your dietary fat, especially saturated fat, with monounsaturated fats. Keep in mind that these healthier fats must replace saturated or polyunsaturated fat in the diet rather than be added to it. In other words, don't increase the total fat content of your meal plan.

Nuts can substitute for animal protein in recipes or be eaten in small servings as snacks. Garnish vegetables with slivered almonds, hazelnuts, or pine nuts instead of butter. Use nut butters (such as peanut, cashew, or almond butter) without partially hydrogenated oils. Avocados can be sliced and added to a sandwich of tomato, sprouts, or other vegetables.

Prepare salad dressings or pastas with olive oil. Cook (sauté, stir-fry, or broil) with small amounts of olive or canola oil. Canola oil is a monounsaturated fat that is less expensive than olive oil and lighter in taste. When you substitute a liquid oil for a solid shortening in a recipe, use 1/4 less oil.

44 What are *trans* fats, and how do they affect my diabetes?

Trans fats are formed in processed foods during hydrogenation. Hydrogenation makes a fat solid when it is at room temperature. For example, liquid vegetable oil is partially hydrogenated to make stick margarine. Partially hydrogenated vegetable oil is used in fried foods, baked products, and snack foods.

Trans fats don't affect blood glucose levels but do increase blood cholesterol levels, which increases your risk for heart disease. If less than 30% of your calories come from fat and 7% from saturated fat, you're probably okay. If you eat a moderately high-fat diet, your *trans* fat intake may be too high.

Food manufacturers are now required to list trans fats on the Nutrition Facts label of food products. While there is no recommended dietary allowance for trans fats, the American Diabetes Association suggests that the intake should be minimized. To minimize *trans* fat intake, don't eat many processed foods. Choose soft table spreads instead of stick margarine. Read food labels and select margarine that has the lowest *trans* fat and saturated fat content and that lists liquid oil as the first ingredient. Look for baked products, convenience dinners, and snack foods with minimal saturated fat and *trans* fat per serving. Use vegetable oil instead of solid shortening in cooking. Check with your RD if you have questions about *trans* fats.

45 Does it matter what kind of margarine and vegetable oil I use?

It depends on the fatty acids they contain—saturated, polyunsaturated, monounsaturated, and *trans* fat. Saturated fats (found in butter and lard) and trans fat (found in partially hydrogenated vegetable oils) are the least healthy. Polyunsaturated fats (corn or soybean oil) are healthier. Monounsaturated fats (canola or olive oil) are the best. All fats are actually mixtures of these three fatty acids.

All margarines are made of vegetable oil. However, the fat is hydrogenated (saturated), so it is less healthy than oil. Tub and squeeze margarines also contain water and air to lower fat and calories. Read the food label to find margarine with only 2 grams of saturated fat per serving and liquid oil as the first ingredient.

Canola and olive oil are the best vegetable oils because they are low in saturated fat and have the largest amount of monounsaturated fats. Safflower, sunflower, corn, and soybean oil are also low in saturated fat.

46 What are fat replacers, and how do they affect my diabetes?

Fat replacers are used to give reduced-calorie foods the texture, appearance, and taste of full-fat products. Most fat replacers are made from carbohydrates and can raise your blood glucose level. The ones made of protein or fat are not as likely to affect blood glucose. Remember that food with a fat replacer can still have lots of calories.

Fat replacers made from carbohydrates include polydextrose, cellulose gum, corn syrup solids, dextrin, maltodextrin, hydrogenated starch hydrolysate, carrageenan, and modified food starch. They combine with water to provide thicker texture, as in fat-free salad dressings. Fat replacers made from protein include Simplesse and whey protein concentrate. They are used in cheese, sour cream, salad dressings, baked goods, butter, and mayonnaise spreads.

Olestra is a fat replacer found in salty snacks. Made from sugar and fat, it does not act like fat. It is not digested, so it contributes no calories. It may cause cramping and diarrhea and may inhibit the absorption of some fat-soluble vitamins.

Check the Nutrition Facts panel for calories and the amount of carbohydrate, fat, and protein in foods with fat replacers. Ask your RD to help you work these foods into your meal plan.

47 What about flaxseed and omega-3 (fish oil) supplements?

Omega-3 fatty acids are polyunsaturated fatty acids with a slightly different structure. These fats are found mostly in seafood, especially in cold-water varieties such as albacore tuna, salmon, mackerel, sardines, and lake trout, but they are also found in flaxseed. Some research suggests that omega-3 fats have beneficial effects in preventing heart disease and lowering certain blood fats in people with type 2 diabetes.

While omega-3 (fish oil) supplements contain omega-3 fatty acids, they are not recommended as a substitute for fish or as a dietary supplement. The safety, effectiveness, and proper dosage of fish oil supplements are not known. Instead, the ADA recommends that you enjoy the benefits of omega-3 fatty acids by including two to three servings of fish per week in your healthy eating plan.

Flax is high in fiber and omega-3 fatty acids and is eaten as flaxseed (whole or ground), flax flour, or flax oil. Flax seeds must be milled into ground flax for the body to obtain the health benefits from the omega-3 fatty acids in the flax oil found in the seeds. Flaxseed can be used in breads or muffins, either ground or as whole seeds, and can be sprinkled over cold or hot cereal.

48 What are plant sterols and stanols, and how do they affect my diabetes?

Plant sterols and stanols are components of plant cell membranes that are structurally similar to cholesterol. These substances appear to interfere with the absorption of cholesterol in the intestine, thereby lowering total and LDL cholesterol in the body. Diets that are low in saturated fat and cholesterol and include approximately two grams per day of plant sterols/ stanols may have beneficial effects on lipid levels.

The FDA has approved the use of plant sterols and stanols in margarine spreads and salad dressing. Two brands currently on the market are Benecol and Take Control. Consuming two to three tablespoons a day of these products can lower LDL cholesterol by about 15% in people who have elevated levels. These spreads are designed for people with elevated cholesterol and have not been shown to prevent high cholesterol in those with normal cholesterol levels. Consult with your doctor or registered dietitian about whether these products would be useful for you.

Chapter 5
How Sweet It Is

49 Does eating sugar cause diabetes?

No. Although diabetes has been called "sugar diabetes" for many years, eating sugar does not cause it. Type 1 diabetes happens when your body's immune system destroys the insulin-producing beta-cells in the pancreas. Factors that may cause the immune system to do this are autoantibodies, cow's milk (see page 131), genes, and oxygen-free radicals (see page 98). Type 1 diabetes is probably triggered by one of these environmental factors in people who have the genes for developing the disease.

Type 2 diabetes is different from type 1. The bodies of most people with type 2 make insulin but can't use it well. Genetics play a strong role in type 2 diabetes, as do age, obesity, and lifestyle. Obese individuals who eat a high-calorie diet and don't participate in physical activity are more likely to develop type 2 diabetes. In this case, too much sugar may provide excess calories, in the same way excess fat does. The resulting weight gain and obesity, which interfere with the action of insulin, can lead to the development of type 2 diabetes.

50 I'm confused about sugars and starches. Which will raise my blood glucose more, a brownie or a piece of bread ?

Sugars and starches are carbohydrates, the nutrient that most directly affects blood glucose levels. For years, we thought that the body absorbed sugar more quickly than starch, and people were told to avoid sweets. It turns out that a small brownie (15 grams of carbohydrate) raises blood glucose about the same amount as one slice of bread (also 15 grams of carbohydrate). Research has shown that sugar is okay for people with diabetes if it is part of a meal plan. It is substituted for other carbohydrate foods rather than eaten in addition to them.

Certain factors affect the way your blood glucose responds to sugars and starches. Both the amount and the type of carbohydrate influence your blood glucose response. When you eat sweets, observe whether other foods are eaten at the same time, how quickly you eat, how the food was prepared, and the amount of protein and fat in the food. Measure your blood glucose 1–2 hours after eating and note the effect sugar has on it. Use this information to make decisions about including sweets in your meal plan.

51 How many grams of sugar am I allowed to eat in a day?

There is no magic number of grams for each day, but eat sugar sparingly. Sugar has calories but few vitamins or minerals. Foods high in sugar may also be high in fat, which can lead to weight gain and make diabetes management more difficult.

The Nutrition Facts label gives the number of grams of sugar in packaged foods. This number includes both natural and added sugars. Natural sugars are found naturally in foods, such as fructose in raisins or lactose in milk. These sugars provide some vitamins and minerals. Added sugars are put into foods to make them sweet, such as sugar in cookies or high fructose corn syrup in soft drinks. These sugars provide calories but no other nutrients.

When you read the food label, check the type of sugar the food contains, but focus on the grams of total carbohydrate rather than the grams of sugar. Sugar and sweets are fine occasionally, in small portions, if you substitute them for other carbohydrate foods in your meal plan and check your blood glucose to see how the food affects you.

52 Are there sweeteners that are free foods? How can I tell which to use?

Yes. "Nonnutritive" sweeteners are free foods because they have no calories or carbohydrate. They don't raise blood glucose levels. None of them are perfect for all uses. Some are great in cold beverages but won't work in baked goods. While the sweeteners themselves are calorie free, don't forget to count the calories, fat, and carbohydrate in the foods they are sweetening.

Neotame is another calorie-free sweetener that the Food and Drug Administration has approved as safe. It can function as a standalone sweetener but works particularly well when blended with other sweeteners. Currently it is primarily used as a manufacturer's food ingredient and is not available for purchase as a tabletop sweetener.

53 What calorie-containing sweeteners can I use instead of sugar?

Sugar and all the other calorie-containing sweeteners provide about the same amount of calories and raise your blood glucose in the same way. Fructose, honey, and other "natural" sweeteners have no advantages over the other sweeteners that contain calories. You can substitute the nutritive sweeteners listed below for other carbohydrates in your meal plan. Remember to count the calories and carbohydrate they contain.

54 Can I eat all I want of food that is labeled "sugar free"?

No. A food labeled sugar free must contain less than 0.5 grams of sugar per serving, but it may have calories and carbohydrate. For example, sugar-free pudding has 0 grams of sugar, but it also has 70 calories and 6 grams of carbohydrate in a 1/2-cup serving. If you were to eat unlimited amounts, you could easily add enough calories and carbohydrate to sabotage your diabetes goals and weight-control efforts over time.

Although the sweetener used in a sugar-free product may be calorie free (such as acesulfame potassium, aspartame, neotame, saccharin, or sucralose), the other ingredients in the food usually contain fat, carbohydrate, protein, and calories. Nonnutritive sweeteners may be used along with other sweeteners that contain calories, so don't rely on the "sugar-free" symbol on the front of the package alone. Read the ingredient list and food label carefully so that you can make the best choices for healthy eating (see page 9).

55 What are sugar alcohols? Will foods with sugar alcohols cause my blood glucose to rise?

Sugar alcohols (also known as polyols) are used to sweeten a variety of foods, such as candy, chewing gum, baked goods, ice cream, and fruit spreads. They are also found in toothpaste, mouthwash, and medications, including cough syrups and throat lozenges. Sugar alcohols have 2–3 calories per gram, compared to 4 calories per gram in other sugars. Sugar alcohols are absorbed more slowly than other sugars and cause a smaller rise in blood glucose levels after they are eaten. If you are counting carbohydrates, you can subtract one-half of the sugar alcohol grams from the total carbohydrate grams in the food to get a more accurate prediction of the food's effect on your blood glucose level.

Because sugar alcohols are not completely digested in the stomach, you may experience side effects such as diarrhea, intestinal cramping, or gas if you eat too much of them. One recommendation is to eat no more than 20–50 grams of sugar alcohol in a day, which is the amount found in 12–33 pieces of sugar alcohol–sweetened hard candy.

The sugar alcohols you'll see on food labels include erythritol, malitol, hydrogenated starch hydrolysate, mannitol, sorbitol, isomalt, xylitol, and lactitol.

56 What is stevia?

Stevia is a sweetener that is 30–300 times sweeter than sugar, but it has no calories. It is made from an herb and comes in three forms. The greenish-black liquid is 70 times sweeter than sugar and is used to sweeten cereal, tea, coffee, and hot chocolate. It's also used in baking but may change the color of foods. The crushed leaf form is 30 times as sweet as sugar. It comes in small tea-bag packets and is sprinkled on cereal and other foods. The leaf particles do not dissolve. The third form of stevia is a white, heat-stable powder that is 300 times sweeter than sugar. The liquid and leaf forms have a slight taste of anise (licorice).

Although it is used in other countries, stevia has not been approved as a food additive by the Food and Drug Administration here. However, health food stores sell it for personal use. There is no research available describing the effects of stevia when used by a person with diabetes. Side effects are also unknown, so discuss the product with your health care team and use caution until more information is available.

57 My aunt told me that high fructose corn syrup in food is what has caused the diabetes epidemic. Is this true? Should I avoid it?

High fructose corn syrup has received much attention as a possible cause of obesity and type 2 diabetes; however, more research is needed to prove a direct correlation. The popular theory is that high fructose corn syrup, particularly in beverages, changes hormonal patterns to favor adding body fat and increasing appetite, leading to obesity. It has not yet been proved that foods sweetened with high fructose corn syrup make any special contribution to obesity, besides the excess calories they contribute. Here are some tips for cutting back on high fructose corn syrup and other added sugars:

- Choose whole fruits over fruit juice and buy only 100% juice rather than fruit drinks, punches, cocktails or "ades."
- Cut back on soda. A 12-oz can of soda contains about 13 teaspoons of sugar in the form of high fructose corn syrup.
- Snack on nuts, cheese, or fresh fruit rather than sweets.
- Have a bowl of low-sugar whole-grain cereal for breakfast instead of a cereal bar, doughnut, or toaster pastry.

Chapter 6
Food and Fitness

58 What kind of exercise burns off enough calories to lose weight?

To lose a pound of body weight you need to burn 3,500 calories—not all at once, but over several days. Most people lose weight by getting more exercise each day and cutting back their food by about 500 calories a day.

The more frequently and more intensely you exercise, the more calories you burn. And exercise includes everyday activities such as vacuuming and gardening. If you are moderately active every day, you will burn about 150 calories, or about 1,000 calories a week. With exercise alone and no diet changes, you would lose 1 pound in 3–4 weeks. A combination of exercise and chores gives you variety.

Number of Calories Burned in 30 Minutes		
Activity	**Body Weight**	
	120 lbs	170 lbs
Aerobic dance	165	230
Bicycling	110	155
Bowling	85	115
Gardening	140	195
Golf (walking)	125	175
Hiking	165	230
Housework	70	95
Mowing lawn	150	215
Swimming, leisurely	165	230
Tennis	195	270
Walking, brisk	110	155

59 Do I need a snack when I exercise?

If you take insulin or oral diabetes medication, whether or not you need a snack depends on your blood glucose level. Check it before and after exercise and during long, hard exercise. (If your blood glucose level is more than 250 mg/dl, do not exercise until it is in your target range.) Use these guidelines before you exercise to determine whether you'll need a snack:

In most cases, if you are managing type 2 diabetes with meal planning and physical activity alone, without medication, you will not need a snack when you exercise.

Type of Exercise	Blood Glucose Level before Exercise	Action
30 minutes, low-intensity (walking)	less than 100 mg/dl	Eat 15 grams of carb.
30–60 minutes, moderate-intensity (tennis, swimming, jogging)	less than 100 mg/dl	Eat 25–50 grams of carb.
	100–180 mg/dl	Eat 10–15 grams of carb.
1–2 hours, strenuous-intensity (basketball, skiing, shoveling snow). At this intense level of exercise, always monitor blood glucose carefully.	less than 100 mg/dl	Eat about 50 grams of carb.
	100–180 mg/dl	Eat 25–50 grams of carb.
	180–250 mg/dl	Eat 10–15 grams of carb.

60 What are some foods or beverages to use with exercise?

If you take insulin or oral diabetes medicine, you may need a snack before, during, or after you exercise. Muscles keep burning glucose even after you stop exercising. It may take the body up to 24 hours to replace glucose stores used during exercise. After strenuous exercise, you may need to monitor your blood glucose every 1–2 hours (see page 74).

When you are exercising, don't wait to be thirsty to drink plenty of fluids. Dehydration can hinder your strength and endurance. Cool water is absorbed faster than warm water. Diluted fruit juice or sports drinks provide carbohydrate and fluids for exercise that lasts more than 1 hour.

Food for Exercise (15 g carbohydrate)	
1 small piece fresh fruit	1/4 cup dried fruit
1 cup yogurt	1/2 English muffin or bagel
2 Tbsp raisins	1/2 cup fruit juice (can be diluted)
4–5 snack crackers	1 small muffin
3 graham crackers	6–8 oz sports drink

61 Can I use sports drinks when I exercise?

Water is the best drink when you're exercising less than 1 hour. Everyone needs carbohydrate during exercise that lasts more than an hour and is of moderate to high intensity (swimming, jogging, soccer, shoveling heavy snow). When muscle stores of fuel are used up, blood glucose supplies the fuel for prolonged exercise. Sports drinks provide fluids, are easy to take, and are easier to digest than food during prolonged exercise. Certain sports drinks are better than others. Drinks with a concentration of carbohydrate or sugars greater than 10% (such as fruit juice and regular soda) may not be absorbed well and may cause cramps, nausea, diarrhea, or bloating. Diluted fruit juice (1/2 water, 1/2 juice) works better.

Name	Portion Size	Calories	Carbo-hydrate (g)	Carbohydrate Concentration (%)
All Sport Body Quencher	8 oz	70	20	8
Exceed Energy Drink Powder	2 Tbsp + 8 oz water	70	17	7
Gatorade Thirst Quencher	8 oz	50	14	6
Power Ade Thirst Quencher	8 oz	70	19	8

62 When should I eat breakfast and take my insulin if I work out early in the morning?

You can exercise before or after breakfast, as long as you check your blood glucose and adjust your insulin if necessary.

- To exercise before breakfast: First check your blood glucose. If it is 100 mg/dl or higher, eat or drink 10–15 grams of carbohydrate and then exercise. If it is lower than 100 mg/dl, add another 10–15 grams of carbohydrate (total of 20–30 grams) and wait 10–15 minutes. Check again, and if it is above 100 mg/dl, go exercise. You may need more carbohydrate during exercise, depending on the type of exercise. After exercise, check your blood glucose again, take your insulin, and eat breakfast. You may need to decrease your usual morning dose of insulin, depending on the time and intensity of exercise.
- To exercise after breakfast: If you work out 1–2 hours after breakfast, eat your usual breakfast. You may need to eat more carbohydrate at breakfast or to adjust your insulin, but you need to keep a record of your blood glucose levels before, during, and after exercise to learn your response to exercise at particular times of the day. This record can help you decide whether food and insulin adjustments are needed.

63 I'm 65. Can I start a weight-training program now? Do I need an amino acid (protein supplement)?

Weight (or resistance) training can give you more strength and endurance for your daily activities and help prevent osteoporosis. Building muscle mass is not just for young people. As you get older, your body loses muscle mass and tone unless you do something about it. Muscle mass burns calories even when you are doing absolutely nothing. So the benefits of weight training go way beyond those you see in the mirror.

If you get serious about weight training, your protein needs are only slightly higher (about 2–4 oz more meat, chicken, or fish a day). Excess protein can actually be harmful by causing dehydration and straining the kidneys. You can get enough amino acids—and all the other essential nutrients that supplements don't supply—from the food you eat. Food also costs less than protein in powder or pill form.

64 How much exercise do I need to stay healthy?

To help you keep your blood glucose levels on target, assist with weight control, and reduce the risk of heart disease, the ADA recommends at least 150 minutes per week of moderate-intensity aerobic physical activity or 90 minutes per week of vigorous aerobic exercise. You should be physically active at lease three days a week, with no more than 2 days in a row without physical activity. Examples of moderate-intensity aerobic exercise are tennis, swimming, or jogging. Vigorous aerobic exercise includes basketball, skiing, and shoveling snow.

Another approach that can help you manage your weight and reach your physical activity goals every day is the "Shape Up America 10,000 Steps Program." In this program you count the number of steps you take every day using a pedometer. The goal is at least 10,000 daily steps from everyday activities in addition to walks or other forms of physical activity such as jogging or running. To find out more visit www. shapeup.org.

Chapter 7
Weighty Issues

65 What is BMI, and why is it important?

Body mass index, or BMI, combines your weight and height into one number. BMI applies to both men and women and is related to total body fat. The risk for type 2 diabetes, high blood pressure, lipid disorders, cardiovascular disease, gallbladder disease, osteoarthritis, sleep apnea, respiratory problems, and cancer rises in people whose BMI is over 25. To find your BMI:

1. Multiply your weight in pounds by 705.
2. Divide your answer by your height in inches.
3. Divide this answer by your height again.

For example, a person who is 5 feet 6 inches tall and weighs 185 pounds has a BMI of about 30.

Another alternative is to use a BMI calculator, such as the one found on the Web site of the National Heart, Lung, and Blood Institute (http://nhlbisupport.com).

Recent guidelines define overweight as a BMI of 25–29.9 and obesity as a BMI of 30 and above. Keep in mind that the BMI is only a guideline. A very muscular, active person could have a high BMI without health risks. On the other hand, a couch potato may have a lower BMI yet have too much body fat.

66 How can I determine my ideal body weight?

There is actually a range of body weights associated with good health. For example, a man or woman who is 5 feet 5 inches tall should weigh between 114 and 150 pounds. You must consider your age, gender, body shape, and the location of your body fat. Talk to your health care providers about the best weight for you.

People with fat around the upper body, waist, and abdomen ("apple" shape) tend to have more health problems than those who put on fat on the lower body, hips, and thighs ("pear" shape). Health problems associated with apple shapes include insulin resistance, higher blood cholesterol, a tendency toward heart and blood vessel disease, and high blood pressure.

To determine your body shape (waist-to-hip ratio):

1. Measure around your waist or 1 inch above your navel.
2. Measure your hips at their biggest point.
3. Divide the waist measurement by the hip measurement.

For a woman, a ratio of greater than 0.8 means an apple shape; a ratio of less than 0.8 means a pear. For a man, a ratio greater than 1.0 means an apple, and a ratio of less than 1.0 means a pear.

67 I need to lose weight to improve my blood glucose levels, but I can't get started. How can I set a reasonable weight loss goal and achieve it?

Setting realistic goals is the key. If you start with a modest weight loss goal of 10–15 pounds, you are more likely to achieve and maintain it. The good news is that a weight loss of as little as 10–15% of your weight can lower your health risks and improve your diabetes management. Once you've reached your first goal, you can assess your progress and set your sights on the next target.

When you have chosen a weight loss goal, these tips can help you get started:

- Write down your goal and keep it where you will be reminded of it each day.
- Share your goal with someone who will see your progress, such as your health care team or a caring friend.
- Take one immediate action to get started. For example, schedule an appointment with an RD or join an exercise class. Taking action improves your chances for success!
- Commit to small daily actions, such as packing a healthy lunch rather than going out for fast food.
- Find new ways to deal with stress, such as taking a walk or doing yoga.

68 Why can some people maintain their weight loss, while others regain every pound?

Researchers have found that people who maintain their weight loss have done certain things to succeed. You can try the following:

- Get help in developing a personalized meal plan that works for you instead of following a preprinted diet from a magazine or book.
- Exercise. Increased physical activity is one of the best ways to keep lost weight from returning.
- Keep records of blood glucose levels, physical activity, and the food you eat.
- Surround yourself with friends or relatives who support your efforts. They help you keep going!
- Stay away from a quick-fix approach and commit to long-term weight control.
- Don't deny yourself. Occasionally eat small portions of your favorite foods.
- Find other ways to cope with everyday problems instead of smoking, sleeping, drinking, or eating too much.
- Do your best, but don't make excuses, pity yourself, or put yourself down if you aren't perfect in your efforts.
- Be upbeat. Believe that you will succeed and attempt to make your life happier and more fulfilling.

69 Help! My meal plan isn't working any more. What am I doing wrong?

It may not be your meal plan. Diabetes and its treatments can affect how you lose weight. People who follow an intensive glucose management plan may gain weight because they start absorbing all the energy from their food, rather than losing calories through urine (see page 31). Blood glucose levels that are near normal are a better measure of health success than the numbers on your scale. Ask yourself:

- Do I have the wrong goal? Your goal is not a certain weight but improved diabetes management. Don't step on the scale too often.
- Can I increase my physical activity? Look for ways to add activity every day—walking more, using stairs instead of elevators.
- Am I snacking on too many fat-free foods? Fat free doesn't mean calorie free. Fruit, cut-up vegetables, and whole grains are better snacks.
- Am I eating a variety of foods? A rigid weight loss plan may keep you from learning how to add variety to your meals. Diet boredom can lead to overeating.
- How are my serving sizes? Too much of a good thing can make a difference in weight and diabetes management (see page 8).

70 I'm having a hard time sticking with my weight loss plan. Are there any quick tips to keep me on the right track?

Here are some tried-and-true tips:

- Keep weight loss goals reasonable. You can't lose 25 pounds, stop smoking, and begin walking 3 miles a day all in one week!
- Set small weight loss targets. Aim for 5-pound goals.
- Record your weight and blood glucose levels. It's encouraging to see improvements in blood glucose, even if your weight doesn't change.
- Periodically, write down what you eat for one day. Measure your serving sizes.
- Drink a large glass of water before every meal.
- Use a smaller plate to "trick" yourself into thinking you have more than enough to eat.
- Eat slowly and stop when you just begin to feel full.
- Put your fork down between mouthfuls and chew thoroughly.
- Keep low-calorie snacks on hand—sugar-free gelatin, cut-up fresh vegetables, and fresh fruit.
- Don't deprive yourself of your favorite food. Cut back on how often you eat it or on your serving size.
- Expect setbacks and don't give up. Begin again tomorrow.

71 Won't skipping meals help me cut back on calories and lose weight?

No. Eating all your calories in one or two big meals can send your blood glucose levels sky-high. Eating smaller meals more often keeps the amount of carbohydrate entering your system small and consistent, so your glucose level stays within your target range. This can keep your weight under control. And you'll need less insulin.

When to eat depends on many factors, particularly the type of diabetes medication you use. If you take insulin, skipping meals can result in dangerous hypoglycemia. Skipping meals can make you hungrier, moody, and unable to focus. This may lead to overeating later in the day. Breakfast-skippers are particularly at risk for grabbing sugary, high-fat foods later in the day (see page 19). Always eat within a few hours of getting up.

Your metabolism slows down when you do not eat. Eating regularly keeps your energy level high and helps your body burn calories. Eating more often doesn't mean that you eat more calories. See an RD to learn to spread your calories throughout the day. You may find that three meals and three snacks work better for you!

72 Won't skipping a few doses of insulin help me lose weight?

If you take too little insulin on purpose, your body will not use all the calories you eat, and this will result in weight loss. However, it is a very dangerous way to lose a few pounds. An inadequate dose of insulin means you will have higher blood glucose levels. This can affect growth and development in children and adolescents. In the short term, high blood glucose levels cause headache, blurred vision, and stomach upset and make you feel tired, hungry, and thirsty. Underdosing insulin puts you at greater risk for ketoacidosis and having to be hospitalized. It can be life-threatening.

Long-term diabetic complications such as nerve damage, kidney damage, and diabetic eye disease are more likely to develop if you deliberately underdose insulin to control your weight. Some researchers have found that people who misuse insulin have a high rate of psychological problems and may have more difficulty dealing with the diagnosis of diabetes.

Don't skip your insulin shot. Stick to a sensible, health-promoting plan of eating and physical activity to lose weight!

73 Will a very-low-calorie diet work for me?

Probably not. They are for people with type 2 diabetes who are extremely obese and at immediate risk for serious health problems. Weight loss on a very-low-calorie diet (VLCD) is rapid, and blood glucose levels fall within a few days of beginning this restrictive way of eating. VLCDs are not for people with type 1 diabetes, because of the risk of hypoglycemia. A person with diabetes and kidney disease should not try a VLCD because of the high-protein content of the diet.

Most VLCDs are based on drinking a beverage or eating very lean meat. These diets are high in protein to prevent muscle tissue from wasting away and are supplemented with vitamins and minerals because so little food is eaten. Because of the side effects, VLCDs should only be used under the supervision of a physician who specializes in the care of people with diabetes and obesity.

Unfortunately, a VLCD program can be costly, and most people regain all the weight they lost within five years. It might jump-start a weight loss effort, but for truly permanent weight loss, you must make lasting changes in your lifestyle.

74 Why can't I just take diet pills to help me lose weight faster?

There is no "magic bullet." To lose weight, you eat less or exercise more—or both. Diet pills are meant to be used along with meal planning and exercise, not in place of them. These pills have side effects and should not be taken without your health care provider's advice. Weight loss medications are not for everyone and cannot be used long term.

Weight loss drugs work by controlling your appetite, increasing your sense of fullness, or changing the absorption of the fat you eat. Pills that control appetite and feelings of fullness act on brain chemicals. They cause you to feel less hungry, making it easier to stick with a low-calorie diet. Side effects include dry mouth, insomnia, jitteriness, and increased heart rate and blood pressure.

Drugs that change fat absorption don't reduce appetite but prevent the absorption of about 30% of the calories from the fat you eat. The fat is lost in the stools, leading to side effects of oily or loose stools and intestinal gas.

75 Will obesity surgery help me lose weight and cure my type 2 diabetes?

Because obesity is a leading cause of type 2 diabetes, there is much interest in surgery as an option for weight loss and for prevention and treatment of type 2 diabetes. There are two main surgical approaches: a bypass, which avoids a section of the absorptive surface of the intestine; and gastric banding, which seals off a large portion of the stomach, making it quite small and easily filled.

In a recent review of weight loss surgery, researchers found that surgery resulted in considerable weight loss and that there was resolution of diabetes in about 70% of patients after bypass. Many obesity surgery studies have also shown improvements in high blood pressure, blood fats, and sleep apnea following surgery. However, it's important to remember that this surgery is not without risks. Complications resulting from surgery occur in approximately 20% of people and include internal bleeding and gastrointestinal problems such as vomiting or acid reflux. Speak with your physician to determine if your level of overweight, diabetes management, and personal needs make you a good candidate for obesity surgery.

Chapter 8
Off the Beaten Path

76 Should I take chromium supplements or can I get enough from foods?

If you eat a balanced and varied diet, you are getting enough chromium. Some ads claim that chromium supplements will help overcome obesity, help the body use insulin better, prevent hypoglycemia, and take away sugar cravings. The body needs chromium to metabolize protein, carbohydrate, and fat and to produce the glucose tolerance factor, which is believed to improve insulin action. The estimated safe and adequate daily dietary intake of chromium is 35 micrograms (mcg) for men and 25 mcg for women—a tiny amount. Chromium is found in brewer's yeast, wheat germ, corn oil, whole-grain cereals, meats, cheese, bran, liver, kidney, oysters, potatoes with the skin left on, peanuts, and peanut butter.

People who may be at risk for chromium deficiency are those who do not eat healthy foods and suffer from malnutrition, who are on total parenteral nutrition, who are pregnant, or whose glucose levels are frequently out of range. There is currently no evidence to show that chromium deficiency rates are different in people with diabetes versus the general population. Supplements are recommended only for people with signs and symptoms of a deficiency, which is difficult to detect. Results from chromium research are not conclusive.

Most chromium supplements contain more than chromium, are poorly absorbed, and are not regulated by the FDA. Chromium supplements can be expensive, using money that might be better spent on healthy foods.

77 I've heard so much about antioxidants. Will taking them help my diabetes?

Antioxidants include vitamins A, C, and E; beta-carotene; and the mineral selenium. They protect the body from harmful substances known as free radicals. Free radicals are by-products of metabolism that disrupt our natural cancer-fighting defenses and destroy important structures such as cell membranes and DNA. High blood glucose helps free radicals form in the body, and free radicals may be involved in diabetes complications. While some research has shown a connection between antioxidants and the prevention of cancer and heart disease, large clinical trials have shown no benefit, and in some cases antioxidant supplements may even have adverse effects.

Your best bet is to eat a variety of foods rich in antioxidants. Food sources of antioxidants include the following:

- Beta-carotene and vitamin A in green leafy vegetables (broccoli, collard greens, kale, spinach) and red, orange, and yellow fruits and vegetables (apricot, cantaloupe, carrots, mango, peach, pumpkin, sweet potato, tomato, watermelon, squash)
- Vitamin C in broccoli, cantaloupe, citrus fruit (orange, grapefruit, lemon), kiwi, potato, red pepper, strawberries, and tomato
- Vitamin E in almonds, nuts, seeds, vegetable oil, and wheat germ
- Selenium in cashews, halibut, meat, oysters, salmon, scallops, and tuna

78 Will a magnesium supplement improve my diabetes management?

Only if you are magnesium deficient. Magnesium deficiency may play a role in causing insulin resistance, carbohydrate intolerance, and hypertension. Low blood levels of magnesium are frequently seen in individuals with type 2 diabetes, but only people at risk for magnesium deficiency need to have a blood test for magnesium levels. People at risk are older individuals; those taking certain diuretics, antibiotics, or anti-cancer medications; and those with alcoholism, chronic malabsorption problems, or a potassium or calcium deficiency. Individuals whose blood glucose levels are frequently out of their target range may benefit from magnesium supplements. Symptoms of magnesium deficiency include loss of appetite, nausea, vomiting, fatigue, and weakness.

The best sources of magnesium are legumes, nuts, whole grains, and green vegetables. The RDA for adult men is 400–420 mg a day; for adult women, it is 310–320 mg daily.

If a blood test shows magnesium deficiency, your doctor will prescribe a supplement. People with kidney disease should only take a magnesium supplement under a doctor's care.

Food (serving)	Magnesium (mg)
Cashews (1 oz)	75
Spinach, boiled (1/2 cup)	75
Peanut butter (2 Tbsp)	50
Black-eyed peas (1/2 cup)	45
Bran flakes (3/4 cup)	40

79 Can vanadium (vanadyl sulfate) supplements improve my blood glucose levels?

We don't know. At this time there is not enough information to say. This trace element is being studied for its effect on insulin sensitivity and its glucose-lowering ability in people with diabetes.

Vanadyl sulfate is marketed in health food stores as a supplement that mimics the effect of insulin in the body, thereby lowering blood glucose levels. Some ads say that it enables some people to use less insulin or to stop taking insulin altogether. Because supplements are not regulated in the same way as drugs in the United States, this type of claim is legal. But little is known about this supplement, and the side effects are unclear. At this time, vanadium is not considered safe to use.

Recommended levels of vanadium have not been determined. If research proved a connection between vanadium and blood glucose levels and insulin action, vanadium would likely be regulated as a drug rather than as a supplement.

80 What is fenugreek? Can it lower blood glucose and cholesterol?

Fenugreek is a plant used since ancient times for managing diabetes and obesity. Its seed is a spice found in Indian, Middle Eastern, and Mediterranean dishes. Fenugreek contains concentrated amounts of soluble and insoluble fiber and can lower blood cholesterol and slow the rise in blood glucose after eating. It is on the "Generally Recognized as Safe Food and Spice List" from the FDA.

Side effects from fenugreek are the same as those from dietary fiber—excess gas, diarrhea, and poor absorption of glucose and fats. Because fenugreek is in the same plant family as chickpeas, peanuts, and green peas, it is best not to take it if you have an allergy to those products. Pregnant women should not use fenugreek because it can cause uterine contractions. Also, fenugreek may not be safe for you if you are taking an anticoagulant, because it affects blood clotting.

Research and safety data on fenugreek are limited. Speak with your health care providers to decide if fenugreek is a suitable product for you.

81 I've heard that folate will reduce my risk of heart attack. Do I need to take a folate supplement every day?

Researchers have identified an elevated homocysteine level as a risk factor for cardiovascular disease. Homocysteine is an amino acid normally found in blood; a deficiency of folate, vitamin B-12, or vitamin B-6 may increase blood levels of homocysteine. Because people with diabetes are at risk for heart and blood vessel disease, it may be wise for you to pay attention to the amount of folate in your diet. The recommended daily amount of folate is 400 mcg. Ask your health care provider and RD whether they recommend a folate supplement for you. If you are interested in increasing the amount of folate you eat, the following list has some of the best food sources:

Food (serving)	Folate (mcg)
Black-eyed peas (1/2 cup)	105
Cooked spinach (1/2 cup)	100
Asparagus (4 spears)	85
Green peas (1/2 cup)	50
Avocado (1/2 cup)	45

82 I heard a news report that said cinnamon lowers blood glucose levels. Should I take a cinnamon capsule every day?

Research has shown some very promising effects of cinnamon on blood glucose and blood lipids. Studies in people with type 2 diabetes taking sulfonylureas found that cinnamon improved fasting blood glucose by 18–29% after 40 days; total cholesterol, low density lipoprotein (LDL), and triglycerides also dropped. After cinnamon was withheld for the next 20 days, fasting blood glucose was still lower than at the start of the study, meaning that cinnamon may have a long-lasting benefit.

The amount of cinnamon used in the study was equivalent to about a half teaspoonful a day. Cinnamon capsules were not studied and may not have the same effect as cinnamon in food, which is considered safe. If you are interested in adding cinnamon to your diet, try mixing it in sugar-free applesauce or using it on toast, being sure to keep track of the amount of carbohydrate the food provides. Check your blood glucose frequently to note the effect of cinnamon on your diabetes management.

Chapter 9
Food for Thought

83 I don't have lots of time to spend shopping for food and making healthy meals. What can I do?

Here are some tips:

- Plan your meals for the week, using your diabetes meal plan as a guide. Do all your grocery shopping at once.
- Make a shopping list and move through the store quickly.
- Grated, chopped, precooked, and presliced foods will save preparation time. For example, use prechopped broccoli florets from the salad bar.
- "Cook once, serve two or three times." Plan to use leftovers. For example, if you are making pasta for a hot dish at supper, cook an extra handful to use in a cold pasta salad tomorrow. Make a pot roast with vegetables on Sunday and plan to use the leftover beef in beef stew, burritos, or vegetable beef soup later in the week.
- Take a few minutes in the morning to assemble a slow-cooker recipe. Your reward: a ready-to-eat meal at the end of the day.
- Take advantage of the time you have on weekends. Cook and bake in large quantities and freeze portions for future meals and snacks.

84 How can I make my favorite recipes lower in fat?

These tips may help:

- Most recipes (except some baked goods) will taste fine if you cut 1/3–1/2 of the butter or oil.
- When baking, substitute 2 egg whites for a whole egg; use fat-free instead of whole milk. Reduced-calorie butter or margarine has too much water to be used for baking. Because fat gives texture to baked goods, decreasing it can be tricky. Try replacing oil, margarine, or butter with apple-sauce. Substitute an equal amount of fruit for fat to retain moisture and flavor. Puréed prunes taste great in chocolate desserts.
- Marinades need acid, such as lemon juice, vinegar, or wine, more than oil for tenderizing.
- Use lower-fat substitutes. Low-fat yogurt replaces sour cream in dips and dressings. Use evaporated fat-free milk instead of heavy cream. Replace half the ground meat in casseroles with mashed beans or cooked brown rice.
- Use butter-flavored spray on cooked vegetables, baked potatoes, or popcorn.
- Cocoa powder gives chocolate flavor without the fat. Use 3 Tbsp unsweetened cocoa powder and 1 Tbsp vegetable oil to replace 1 oz unsweetened chocolate.

85 How can I eat right on a lean budget?

You don't need expensive diabetic or sugar-free foods. The foundation foods of your meal plan are inexpensive—beans, rice, and whole-grain breads. Here are some other suggestions:

- Fresh vegetables in season are a great buy. Otherwise, canned, fresh, and frozen vegetables are all quite similar nutritionally. Or you can grow or pick your own!
- Buy fruits in season for best taste and bargain prices. Try the local farmer's market. Think about the cost per serving—if apples and melon are the same price per pound, buy the apples. You throw away the rind of the melon, getting less fruit for the price.
- Use fat-free dry milk for cooking and baking. It's inexpensive and stays fresh for a long time if the box is refrigerated. Preshredded cheese saves time but costs more. Buy cheese in blocks and grate it yourself. Buy or make plain yogurt and add your own fresh fruit.
- Make meat a side dish rather than the whole meal. Enjoy meatless meals several times a week. Use leftovers wisely.
- For snacks, try popcorn, pretzels, and cereal.

Choosing fats, sweets, and alcohol less often will be good for your diabetes and your budget.

86 Which frozen dessert is best for me?

You can eat frozen desserts occasionally if you substitute them for other carbohydrates in your meal plan. The following information can help you choose:

- Watch the serving size (1/2 cup). If you eat more, double or triple the nutrient information to keep your count accurate.
- Watch the fat content, particularly the saturated fat. Light ice cream or yogurt contains about half the fat of the regular kind. Fat-free ice cream still has sugar, carbohydrate, and calories.
- A no-sugar-added frozen dessert may still contain carbohydrate, fat, and calories. Sweeteners commonly used in frozen desserts include aspartame and sugar alcohols such as sorbitol (see page 67).
- Check your blood glucose two hours after eating a frozen dessert to see how it affects you.

87 Are frozen dinners a good choice for quick meals?

Frozen dinners have come a long way, but keep the following tips in mind:

- Check the Nutrition Facts panel for the amount of fat and sodium. You want no more than 30% of calories from fat, 10% of calories from saturated fat, and 200 mg of sodium for every 100 calories.
- Most "healthy" frozen dinners are based on small servings. If your meal plan calls for 1,500 calories a day, don't skimp by eating a meal with less than 400 or 500 calories. You'll find yourself hungry later and may overeat on snacks.
- Be aware that although most healthy frozen dinners contain fruits and vegetables, the serving size of these foods is as small as 1 tablespoon in some cases.

You can improve a frozen dinner by adding a salad, some steamed vegetables, and a piece of fruit. It may be better to make your own frozen dinners by putting the extras from home-cooked meals onto microwave-safe dishes in your serving sizes.

88 Are eggs off-limits now that I have diabetes?

No. Contrary to the widely held belief that cholesterol-rich eggs are bad for heart health, several research studies have found that for most people, dietary cholesterol has little effect on the cholesterol level in blood. Saturated fat has a more significant effect on your blood cholesterol level (see page 49). A person's response to dietary cholesterol is highly individual and genetically determined. About 20% of us have little or no response to dietary cholesterol, 50% show a small response, and the remaining 30% are responders, particularly sensitive to high-cholesterol foods. There is no easy test to determine who is cholesterol sensitive, so just be cautious when using eggs and other cholesterol-rich foods.

An egg is an economical source of protein, providing 70 calories, less than 1 gram of carbohydrate, 4.5 grams of fat, and 1 gram of saturated fat. One egg contains vitamins, minerals, and about 215 mg of cholesterol.

Don't eliminate eggs from your diet. Use them wisely or follow the American Heart Association guideline: If you do choose to eat an egg, use a small or medium egg. Remember to balance the dietary cholesterol in the egg with the other foods you eat that day to stay within the recommended intake of 300 mg of cholesterol daily.

89 How can I use herbs and spices?

Herbs and spices taste good, smell good, and best of all, have no effect on diabetes management. They are free foods on every meal plan. Herbs and spices come fresh or dried. Dried herbs have a more intense flavor. (When substituting fresh for dried herbs, double or triple the amount.) The amount of herb or spice that you use in a recipe depends on individual taste. Here is a list of traditional spice partners:

- Beef: bay leaf, chives, garlic, marjoram, savory
- Lamb: garlic, marjoram, mint, oregano, rosemary, sage, savory
- Pork: cilantro, cumin, ginger, sage, thyme
- Poultry: garlic, oregano, rosemary, sage, thyme
- Seafood: chervil, dill weed, fennel, tarragon, parsley
- Pasta: basil, oregano, fennel, garlic, paprika, parsley, sage
- Rice: marjoram, parsley, tarragon, thyme, turmeric
- Potatoes: chives, garlic, paprika, parsley, rosemary
- Fruits: cinnamon, cloves, ginger, mint
- Salads: basil, chervil, chives, dill weed, marjoram, mint, oregano, parsley, tarragon, thyme

Be aware that some herb blends contain sodium or are salts, such as garlic salt or lemon pepper.

Chapter 10
Special
Situations

90 What should I use to treat low blood glucose?

Always carry something with you to treat low blood glucose. Do not use chocolate or candy bars because they may not bring your blood glucose up quickly enough.

1. Check your blood glucose. If it is below 70 mg/ dl or you have signs of hypoglycemia but cannot test, eat one of the foods below.
2. Rest for 15 minutes and retest your blood glucose.
3. If it is still low, eat another treatment food and retest. If it is normal, go to the next step.
4. After treating your low blood glucose, eat an extra snack with about 15 grams of carbohydrate. If a meal or snack is scheduled within an hour, go ahead and eat it now.
5. Get help immediately if your blood glucose is still low after 30 minutes and 2 treatments.

Low Blood Glucose Treatment Foods (15 g carbohydrate)	
1/2 cup juice or regular soft drink	3 pieces of hard candy
10 jelly beans	Glucose or dextrose tablets or gel
8 LifeSavers	4 tsp sugar
1 Tbsp honey	2 Tbsp raisins

91 What foods can I eat when I am sick?

When you are sick, take your usual medication, check your blood glucose, and test your urine for ketones. If you can't eat regular food, have carbohydrates in liquids or soft foods. Drink plenty of fluids, at least 4–6 oz every hour. If you can't eat at your usual times, have 15 g carbohydrate every hour to keep blood glucose from dropping (see list below). These tips can help you handle sick days:

- Sip clear liquids, such as apple juice, sports drinks, or regular soda, if you can't keep anything else down.
- Use broth, vegetable juices, and sports drinks to replace potassium and sodium lost from diarrhea and vomiting.
- Be prepared! Ask your RD for sick-day meal plans.

Sick-Day Foods (15 g carbohydrate)	
1 cup broth soup	1/3 cup plain pudding
1 cup cream soup	1/2 cup ice milk or ice cream
1/2 cup fruit juice	1/2 cup regular gelatin
1 cup milk or yogurt	1/4 cup sherbet
1/2 cup regular soda	1 small frozen juice bar
1 cup sports drink	6 saltines
1/2 cup unsweetened applesauce	

92 Can I safely drink alcohol?

It depends. Alcohol can make blood glucose too high or too low. Eat a meal when you drink alcohol to prevent low blood glucose. Alcoholic beverages with mixers, wine, and beer have carbohydrates and can cause your blood glucose to go too high. Choose lower-calorie mixers such as mineral water, club soda, diet tonic water, diet soda, coffee, or tomato juice. Choose light beer or a glass of wine.

If your blood glucose levels are on target, you may have a moderate amount of alcohol—one drink each day for women, two for men. One drink is 12 oz of beer, 5 oz of wine, or 1 1/2 oz of liquor. If you have type 1 diabetes and you are not overweight, this serving would be an addition to your meal plan. If you have type 2 diabetes or are overweight, any alcohol you drink should be substituted for another food in your meal plan. Ask your RD for help.

Avoid alcohol if your blood glucose levels are not on target, you have an empty stomach, you are pregnant, you have neuropathy, you have problems with alcohol abuse, you take prescription or over-the-counter medications that react with alcohol, or you have just had vigorous exercise.

93 How can I eat less fat when I eat out in restaurants?

Identify your habits by answering these questions:

- How often do you eat out?
- What meals do you eat out most often?
- What type of restaurants do you choose most often?
- What foods do you order?

Select restaurants that have some lower-fat choices. Get copies of menus and decide what you will eat before you arrive. Plan ways to balance your restaurant meal with food choices the rest of the day. Save fat choices for your meal out.

Choose menu items or foods that are baked, braised, broiled, grilled, poached, roasted, steamed, or stir-fried instead of au gratin, fried, breaded, buttered, creamed, sautéed, scalloped, or served with gravy or thick sauce. Look for menu items called light or lean. Ask about food preparation and ingredients. Ask that sauces and salad dressings be served on the side. Decline any extra bread or tortilla chips.

If a serving seems too big, order an appetizer instead, split a main dish with your dining companion, or take home leftovers. Set aside the portion you want to take home as soon as the food arrives.

94 Which fast foods can I eat?

The following tips can help you decide:

- Watch the serving size. Order a regular serving or split the super-size with someone.
- Most restaurants have free nutrient information. Ask for it.
- Go for grilled, broiled, baked, or rotisserie sandwiches. Skip meats with breading and added cheese.
- Remember your fruits and vegetables. Order juice or fruit, a salad or raw vegetables, tomato slices or vegetables for sandwiches, vegetable toppings for potatoes, or vegetables on pizza.
- Bagels, muffins, French fries, baked potatoes, and sandwich buns can be extra large and can give you too much carbohydrate. Cut them in half or split an order.
- Low-fat frozen yogurt, low-fat milk shakes, and fresh fruit are good dessert choices. Order small sizes or share.
- For breakfast, order cereal, English muffins, fruit, and milk.
- Ask that ketchup, barbecue sauce, mayonnaise, salad dressing, tartar sauce, honey, cream cheese, and other sauces be left off your sandwich or salad.

95 How can I avoid overeating at a salad bar or buffet?

A plate from the salad bar can give you more than 1,000 calories, depending on choices and portions. Consider these tips:

- Don't go to restaurants that only offer buffet-style eating or a salad bar.
- Take a stroll around the salad bar, breakfast bar, or buffet to size up your choices before you decide.
- If you are tempted to overdo, use a smaller plate. Single trips are usually less expensive.
- Enjoy plenty of vegetables, legumes (such as kidney and garbanzo beans), and fresh fruit.
- Dark green leafy vegetables (such as spinach and romaine) supply more vitamins than iceberg lettuce. Choose fresh fruit instead of juice or sweet breads at breakfast bars.
- Become familiar with calories and fat in typical salad bar foods. A 2-Tbsp ladle of salad dressing adds 150 calories to a salad. Choose low-fat or fat-free salad dressing.
- Side dishes such as potato salad, pasta salad, and creamy soups add calories and fat quickly. Avoid these or take small servings of less than 1 Tbsp.

96 What do I do if my meal is delayed for an hour?

Don't let your blood glucose get too low. If your scheduled meal is delayed for an hour, take your diabetes medication at your usual time before the meal. Then eat 15 g of carbohydrate at your usual mealtime. Always keep quick and easy carbohydrate foods (see ideas below) with you in your purse, brief-case, locker, glove compartment, or backpack. Eat your dinner when it is ready.

For meals that are delayed for more than 1 1/2 hours, adjustments depend on when and what kind of diabetes medications you take. Many times you can switch a snack with a meal. Check with your diabetes professionals for a specific plan.

Emergency Foods (15 g carbohydrate)	
6 saltines	1/2 oz dried fruit
2 rice cakes	3 prunes
3/4 oz pretzels	3 graham crackers
Cereal bars (may be more than 15 g)	

97 How can I eat healthfully when I travel on the airlines?

The following tips should help:

- If the airline meal won't fit your meal plan, bring your own. Having food with you is essential for any kind of travel.
- If a meal is to be served, call your agent or airline several days before the flight and order a special meal. Major airlines offer diabetic, vegetarian, low-calorie, low-fat, and low-sodium meals. When you board, tell the flight attendant that you ordered a special meal and that you need it on time. After your meal arrives, take your diabetes medication. If your special meal isn't available, eat the regular meal and substitute other food that you have brought. Foods such as bagels, cereal, fruit, crackers, cheese, raisins, and bottled water travel easily.
- Drink plenty of liquids before, during, and after the flight to avoid dehydration and jet lag. Beverage choices include milk, vegetable and fruit juice, and bottled water. Don't drink too many caffeinated beverages.
- Check your blood glucose. Your activity level during airline travel is low, so you may need to adjust your meal plan or medication. For help, contact your RD.

98 How can I manage my weight and blood glucose levels during the holiday season?

You can keep your holiday spirit by using the following tips:

- Holiday meals: Thanksgiving dinner can add up to 4,500 calories if you include appetizers, eggnog, turkey, trimmings, and dessert. Redesign dinner with delicious lower-fat dishes. Serve grain, fruit, and vegetable dishes. Substitute white turkey meat for dark meat, make your own cranberry sauce, and skim the fat off the gravy.
- Holiday parties: Have a small snack before you go. Don't socialize by the food table, but do socialize. For potlucks, bring a dish you know you can enjoy. Watch the alcohol; it can lower your resistance to tempting treats.
- Holiday travel: Pack healthy, portable snacks to see you through the trip. Good ones include fresh or dried fruit, pretzels, low-fat chips, ready-to-eat cereal, and low-fat cheese (see page 124).

Take advantage of opportunities for exercise. Walk the mall before you shop or take a stroll with your family after dinner to see neighborhood decorations. Keep things in perspective, and if you overindulge, make good choices the rest of the year.

99 How do I adjust food and insulin for a swing-shift schedule?

Your RD and physician must help you plan insulin doses, mealtimes, and physical activities. Multiple daily injections are usually recommended. Learning to adjust rapid-acting insulin to your meal size and carbohydrate content (see pages 17 and 34) gives you flexibility for unpredictable meals. Frequent blood glucose monitoring on workdays and days off helps you make adjustments. Your activity varies from workdays to days off, so your food and/or insulin need adjustments then, too.

If you work the 11:00 p.m.–7:00 a.m. shift, try this schedule:

1. Eat before you go to work and take rapid-acting insulin and intermediate- or long-acting insulin (usual before-breakfast injections).
2. Eat your next meal around 3:00 a.m. and take rapid-acting insulin.
3. Eat a snack, if needed, between 3:00 and 7:00 a.m.
4. Eat a meal at home between 8:00 and 8:30 a.m. and take rapid-acting insulin and intermediate- or long-acting insulin (usual before-dinner injections).
5. Sleep between 9:00 a.m. and 4:00 p.m.
6. Eat a snack between 5:00 and 8:00 p.m.

100 Should I use a slow-release carbohydrate snack bar to prevent hypoglycemia?

Products such as Extend Bar and Nite Bite are medical foods that reduce hypoglycemia for hours, particularly at night. These snack bars are based on a long-acting carbohydrate (such as cornstarch) and come in fruit flavors, chocolate crunch, and peanut butter.

These bars were developed when researchers found that children with glycogen storage disease and hypoglycemia who ate uncooked cornstarch had stable blood glucose levels for nine hours. The same was true in children with diabetes who followed an intensive insulin regimen. Snack bars were created as a tasty alternative to plain cornstarch.

The Diabetes Control and Complications Trial (DCCT) showed that hypoglycemia accompanies intensive diabetes management. If you are taking multiple daily insulin injections, these bars may help you. They contain 22 grams of carbohydrate per bar (1 1/2 starch exchanges) and are added to an evening snack to reduce the risk of nighttime and early-morning hypoglycemia. Blood glucose monitoring can help you determine the effect these snack bars have on you. Consider the cost and taste and discuss using slow-release carbohydrate snack bars with your diabetes care providers.

101 Do I need to drink a nutritional supplement now that I'm a senior?

Maybe. For some people, keeping a balance of nutrients may be more difficult because calorie needs decrease with aging, food budgets get tight, appetite decreases, social contact is reduced, or eating problems arise.

If you are in good health and have a varied diet, you probably don't need these supplement drinks. However, there are drinks and shakes designed specifically for people with diabetes, such as Glucerna and Choice dm, and many people use them simply for convenience. Check the Nutrition Facts panel for calories, carbohydrate, protein, and fat content. Some are high in sugar. Ask your RD whether these drinks fit your meal plan. Monitor your blood glucose levels when you use these nutrition drinks to see how they affect your diabetes. You may not be able to find these products in stores near you, or they may be too expensive for your budget. Ask your RD about supplemental drinks you can make at home. If you are concerned about being underweight, ask for high-calorie meal ideas, too. Try eating five or six small meals a day.

Chapter 11
Nutrition Potpourri

102 Is there a relationship between cow's milk and type 1 diabetes?

The answer remains a mystery. Researchers are studying early exposure to cow's milk (before age 3–4 months) as a cause of type 1 diabetes. Infant formulas are made from cow's milk. Children with type 1 diabetes have shown higher amounts of antibodies that recognize a specific protein in cow's milk. The immune response to the milk proteins might be related to the destruction of insulin-producing beta-cells in the pancreas and to type 1 diabetes. Other studies have not found this same link between cow's milk and type 1 diabetes.

Breast milk is the best source of nutrition during the first year of life for infants with or without diabetes. Breast milk offers physical, emotional, and practical benefits. The baby benefits even when breastfed for only a short time.

However, breastfeeding may not be right for every woman. Commercial infant formula is a healthful alternative or supplement to breastfeeding. The cow's milk used to make infant formula has been modified to meet an infant's special needs. The decision to breastfeed or to use commercial infant formula is a personal one. Discuss questions or concerns with your diabetes professionals and your pediatrician.

103 Will becoming a vegetarian help my diabetes management?

A vegetarian food plan, combined with carbohydrate counting, can be a healthy choice for people with diabetes. There are several types of vegetarian diets.

- Lacto-ovo-vegetarian: no flesh foods, including meat, fish, seafood, poultry, and their by-products, but includes some dairy products and eggs
- Lacto-vegetarian: no flesh foods, eggs, and their by-products, but includes some dairy products
- Vegan: no foods of animal origin

Vegetarian meal plans are based on fruits, vegetables, grains, beans, lentils, soybeans, nuts, and seeds. As a result, they are low in fat, cholesterol, and calories. Decreasing your use of animal products offers you several diabetes health advantages. Vegetarians are less likely to be overweight, have high cholesterol levels, or have high blood pressure. They are also less likely to suffer from heart and blood vessel disease and certain cancers. If you have type 1 diabetes, becoming a vegetarian may enable you to use less insulin. If you have type 2 diabetes, the weight loss from a vegetarian meal plan may improve your blood glucose levels. An RD can help you plan vegetarian meals and ensure that you get all the protein, calcium, vitamin B-12, vitamin D, iron, and omega-3 fatty acids you need.

104 I binge-eat under stress. How can I avoid overeating the next time I feel pressured?

Learn the difference between hunger and appetite. Hunger is a physical sensation that tells you that your body needs food. Appetite comes from the mind and is triggered by sensation and emotion. The following are several ways to deal with the urge to "stuff your feelings" or binge:

- Identify the situations that cause you to overeat. Keep a diary of how much you eat, when you eat, and what the triggers are.
- Establish regular eating patterns. Skipping meals or not eating enough leads to overeating.
- Limit foods that tempt you. If it's chocolate, don't bring full-sized candy bars into the house; a fun-sized bar may satisfy the craving.
- Change the ways you cope with stress. Rather than eat, exercise. Being active (walking, biking) is good for your mind and your body. Talk with a supportive friend or family member. Enjoy a warm bath or long shower.
- Take good care of yourself. Listen to music, go to a movie, or get a massage.

Stress can affect your blood glucose in several ways. Discuss your reactions to stress with your health care team. If you are having trouble with binge eating, ask your team for a referral to a counselor or psychologist for help.

105 Should I follow a low-sodium diet?

The recommended sodium intake for people with diabetes is less than 2,400 mg per day. People with high blood pressure and kidney disease should eat less than 2,000 mg per day.

While most people aren't affected by excess sodium, some are. If you are among the 30% of Americans who have sodium-sensitive blood pressure, decreasing sodium intake will reduce your blood pressure.

The DASH (Dietary Approaches to Stop Hypertension) diet eating plan has been proven to lower blood pressure without medication in just 14 days. The DASH diet involves eating more fruits and vegetables, along with low-fat or nonfat dairy products. To learn more about the DASH eating plan, visit the Web site of the National Heart, Lung, and Blood Institute at www. nhlbi.nih.gov.

Tips for Lowering Your Sodium Intake

- Check the Nutrition Facts label for sodium content.
- Buy fresh meats, fruits, and vegetables instead of high-salt meat products (bacon, cold cuts, ham), canned soups, or frozen dinners.
- Be cautious with condiments and sauces. Cut back on pickles, ketchup, soy sauce, salad dressing, steak sauce, and teriyaki sauce.
- Cook with less salt. Try herbs, spices, lemon juice, pepper, or garlic (see p. 113).
- Remove the salt shaker from the table. Taste food before salting.
- When dining out, avoid high-sodium menu items. Recognize them by their description (smoked or in broth). Keep your order simple (without sauces or fillings) and request that it be prepared without added salt.

106 I have gastroparesis. What changes do I make in my diet?

As a result of diabetes nerve damage, your stomach has lost the ability to churn food into small pieces, and food stays in the stomach too long. Symptoms include nausea, vomiting, weight loss, and a feeling of bloating and fullness. Your blood glucose level may be difficult to manage because food is not delivered to the small intestine for absorption in time to match the diabetes medication you take. You may need medication that stimulates your stomach to contract and empty.

As for your diet, you may need to:

- Eat small meals over the day rather than one or two large meals.
- Avoid fatty foods, because fat slows stomach emptying.
- Avoid foods that are difficult to digest, such as legumes, lentils, and citrus fruits.

Because high blood glucose levels can also slow stomach emptying, getting your blood glucose levels on target is an important part of treatment. If you are taking insulin, your diabetes team may suggest intensive insulin therapy (an insulin pump or three or more injections a day) and frequent blood glucose monitoring. You may need to take your insulin after you eat because of the unpredictability of food absorption.

107 My father has type 2 diabetes, and I'm worried I will get it, too. Is there a diet I can follow to prevent getting diabetes?

Yes, a healthy meal plan with regular physical activity. Type 2 diabetes is probably caused by a hereditary defect that reduces a person's sensitivity to insulin. You can't change that, but you can change the lifestyle habits (high-calorie diet and being inactive and sedentary) that can lead to obesity, which is the most important environmental trigger of type 2 diabetes. This is why healthy eating and exercise are the major parts of prevention and treatment.

The Diabetes Prevention Program (DPP) studied the effects of lifestyle changes and medication on preventing or delaying the development of type 2 diabetes. Participants in the intensive lifestyle group followed a healthy, low-fat diet and exercised at least 150 minutes a week to achieve a weight loss of at least 7% of body weight. These lifestyle changes were nearly twice as effective as medication (58% vs. 31%) in preventing diabetes.

Modest weight loss (5–10% of your body weight) and physical activity (30 minutes daily) are your goals. Talk with your health care providers about starting a low-fat diet and increasing your physical activity. An RD can help you learn about healthy eating and your exercise program.

108 I know what I need to do to eat healthfully, but for some reason I just can't do it. How can I change my eating behaviors?

Healthy eating is an important and challenging self-care behavior that will improve your blood glucose levels. The way you choose your food and why you eat as you do are deeply embedded habits that are difficult to change. Recognize that learning about making healthier food choices takes time, but the extra effort will help you achieve your goals for improved diabetes management and overall health.

Setting goals is a proven strategy that can help you make eating behavior changes. Goals are based on small, measurable steps that you can successfully achieve. Losing 50 pounds may be your ultimate target, but to be successful, you should make your goal as specific as possible. Set small goals such as using the stairs instead of the elevator at your workplace five days a week or eating baked chips rather than French fries at lunch on the weekend.

The SMART Way to Design Your Goals

Specific
Measurable
Achievable
Relevant
Timely

An RD with expertise in diabetes can work with you to set behavior change goals and make an individualized healthy eating plan.

109 Is the glycemic index a good diet for me?

The glycemic index is a method of measuring how different carbohydrate-containing foods affect your postprandial (after eating) blood glucose. Foods that break down quickly during digestion cause a rapid increase in blood glucose, followed by a rapid decrease; foods that break down slowly produce a steady, less steep increase coupled with a slower, extended decrease. For example, baked beans take longer to digest than baked potatoes. Baked beans have a low glycemic index of 38 while baked potatoes have a high glycemic index of 85.

Researchers have concluded that using glycemic index information when planning meals can provide an additional benefit over focusing only on total carbohydrate intake. However, don't make food choices based on their glycemic index alone. Because they contain fat, potato chips and French fries have a lower glycemic index than baked potatoes, but that does not mean you should always choose chips and fries.

Whether the food contains fat or fiber, whether it is cooked or raw, and whether it is whole or has been juiced or mashed also affect the food's glycemic index number. Checking your blood glucose before and after meals will help you evaluate the use of the glycemic index in diabetes meal planning.